Planting *for a* Year of FLOWERS

Grow Your Garden Through the Year

JANE MOORE

Planting *for a* Year of FLOWERS

Grow Your Garden Through the Year

JANE MOORE

Illustrations by James Weston Lewis

Quadrille

For my mother, Theo,
and my two grandmothers,
Jessie and Kitty

Contents

Introduction

This book has been such a joy to write, but there are so many flowers that could have found their way into it, and many that you will wonder why they haven't featured. No rhododendrons? Lacking in lilies! And not a mention of garden favourites such as delphiniums or hollyhocks.

Deciding on just 52 flowers to see a garden through a year of flowering was agonizing, with multiple lists and helpful suggestions from my mum and others. In the end I chose the flowers that I love, those good all-rounders that reward your efforts but don't require anything too demanding in their care. Some are firm personal favourites, others less so, but they are all plants that will provide reliable blooms through the seasons for gardeners everywhere.

The seasons don't follow exact timings; they tend to merge together, and plants do the same, often flowering earlier or longer than expected. So these seasonal guides are a loose grouping, with some flowers, such as peonies, crossing over from spring into summer, and others, like Michaelmas daisies, often blooming in summer but also providing a glorious show in the early golden days of autumn.

Do bear in mind that this is, above all, a book about flowers. Nonetheless, I have tried to include a mixture of plants: a few flowering trees, some invaluable climbers and a handful of shrubs. Most of us will only have room for a few larger plants, and the mainstays of our gardens are herbaceous perennials, annuals and bulbs. These make up the largest number of flowers in this book, and, while I could only include a small number of suggested varieties, I'm certain you'll have fun looking for your own favourites, as well as mine.

How to use this book

While each chapter is broadly separated into seasons, remember that plants don't necessarily flower exactly when they are supposed to. Neither can you guarantee that March, although ostensibly spring, will bring an end to the sudden frosts of winter.

Within each chapter, all the plants listed will flower reliably within that season, some towards the start of the season, others towards the end, and some wonderful ones, like the hardy geranium 'Rozanne' (see page 73), will flower all the way through. The layout of each flower is aimed at giving its key features available at a glance, including the plant type, for example, bulb or shrub; their colour or colours; height; flowering time; and so on.

There are also some quick ideas on planting possibilities and growing conditions, so you can include or dismiss them before you go any further. For example, if you're looking for a plant to grow under your apple tree, you don't want something that needs full sun and light soil.

The broader description of each flower and its garden use is aimed at giving ideas on how and where it could be planted in the garden for best effect, and highlights good varieties. Some of the more popular plants – such as daffodils, tulips, dahlias and roses – have been treated to an in-depth profile, expanding on suggestions for planting combinations and detailing some of my favourite varieties.

For many plants, propagation is as easy as sowing a few seeds or taking a cutting, but some require more specialist skills. For example, many trees, climbers and roses are often grown by grafting a chosen variety onto a different rootstock. Propagating these by cuttings is entirely possible, but they may not become strong, robust plants, so propagation is best left to the professionals.

I've highlighted those plants that are especially beneficial to wildlife, giving each plant a grade of 1 to 5 (5 being the most valuable to wildlife and 1 the least). Please note that all plants will offer habitats and refuge for wildlife and that bees will visit whatever plant is in flower, as long as it produces pollen.

Finally, I've added a fascinating fact for each flower. With so many of these plants, it was a question of picking just one story, as the world of plants is full of fascinating facts, stories, history and folklore.

Essential gardening kit

A handful of good tools makes for happy and successful gardening. You don't need many, but what you do use should be well-made, sturdy and, above all, comfortable to work with. Make sure your spade or rake is the correct height and weight for you to use easily and comfortably, as the right fit will encourage you to get out in the garden, sowing, planting and savouring a long season of flowers.

SPADE

A spade is a very personal tool. I have a couple of spades, including one with a narrow, very sharp blade, which is ideal for splitting clumps of herbaceous plants. Choose carefully, considering whether you'll be digging over large beds or simply moving plants around your borders from time to time.

BORDER FORK

I much prefer a border fork, with its smaller head and close-together tines, to its larger cousin, the standard garden fork. With a narrow border fork, you can squeeze in between plants, tickling the soil to prevent it from capping over, which allows rain to penetrate down to the plant's roots.

SECATEURS

These are essential and you'll pick them up every time you go into the garden. Whether you're doing a quick spot of deadheading, cutting a few flowers for a vase, or pruning your roses, a good pair of secateurs makes light work. Buy a good-quality pair and they will last you a lifetime, especially if you look after them.

LOPPERS

Where the secateurs leave off, the loppers step in, making pruning thicker stems a cinch. As with secateurs, buy a quality pair and keep them clean, well-oiled and sharp.

TROWEL

A decent trowel with a pointed tip and a good scoop is a tool with multiple uses. Use it for scooping out compost, planting delicate seedlings or weeding out stubborn weeds. Some trowels have a measuring stick marked on them, which can be useful when planting bulbs.

GLOVES

A strong pair of gloves is essential for dealing with prickly weeds such as brambles, as well as pruning roses and clearing up afterwards. I like a thin, tactile pair for lighter work, such as weeding, and a tougher, thicker pair for those pesky thistles.

WATERING CAN

It's worth investing in a good watering can, as they're often made from more robust materials and are nicely balanced when full. Watering cans are great for targeting water exactly where it's needed, and one with a good rose (nozzle) is vital for watering delicate seedlings.

Glossary of gardening terms

ANNUAL: A plant that grows from seed, flowers, sets its own seed and dies, all in one growing season.

BIENNIAL: A plant that grows from seed in its first year, producing only leaves. In its second year, it flowers and sets seed before dying.

BULB: A modified stem of a plant that stores nutrients in its layered leaves and from which the plant grows, examples include tulips and onions. When bought, bulbs are a plant in the dormant or resting stage of their cycle.

CORM: Much the same as a bulb, except it is solid and stores nutrients in its stem. Examples include crocuses and gladioli.

CUTTING: A piece of a plant that is cut off to create a new plant. Cuttings can be softwood, when the plant stems are soft; semi-ripe, when they are firmer later in the season; hardwood, when the stems are firm and woody; or root cuttings, where a piece of the root is used.

DIVISION: A method of creating new plants where a plant is divided into smaller pieces, each with a section of growing crown and root.

HALF HARDY: A plant able to grow outdoors at all times except in sharp frosts.

HARDY: A plant that can withstand the frosts and cold weather without dying.

LAYERING: A method of propagation where the stem is left attached to the plant, weighted down and encourage to root. Once rooted, it can be cut from the parent plant.

MULCH: A layer of bulky organic material that is placed around the base of a plant.

PERENNIAL: A plant that lives for three years or more.

SHRUB: A small to medium- sized woody plant that branches from the base of the plant.

TREE: A tall, woody plant, usually with a single trunk.

GRAFTING: The joining of one plant to a different rootstock to enhance the vigour, qualities and health of the overall plant.

DEADHEADING: The simple process of removing finished flowers to prevent them producing seeds. This will keep the plant flowering for a longer period.

TOP DRESSING: Adding a mulch or similar material to the top of the soil to conserve moisture and add nutrients.

OVERWINTERING: Some plants can survive through the winter period, bursting back into growth once the weather warms up in spring. Not all will necessarily survive this period of overwintering.

HEEL CUTTINGS: A propagation technique where the cutting is taken from the parent plant by tearing off a small side shoot with part of the parent stem still attached, called the heel. This is then trimmed to tidy it before inserting the cutting.

F1 HYBRIDS: These are the product of cross pollinating two breeding lines of the same plant chosen for their desirable characteristics. This results in improved health, vigour and disease resistance, as well as uniformity. The drawbacks are that seed is often expensive, the plants can be sterile, and if any viable seed is produced, the resulting plants will be variable, having characteristics of both parent plants.

Spring

Of all the seasons, spring is the one that gets me skipping out into the garden because something has sprung to life overnight. It's a joy to get outside on those early spring days when you can really feel the warmth of the sun, with bulbs in flower, plants flourishing and leaves unfurling daily. Everything moves very swiftly in spring – the difference from early to late spring is like night turning into day. One moment I'm thankful for those first early daffodils, their sunshine heads nodding under the bare branches of the cherry tree; the next, the cherry blossom is creating a canopy of confetti overhead, and the wisteria is festooned with its wonderfully fragrant flowers that are positively irresistible to bees. I'm not alone in the garden, either; all around there are the sounds of buzzing insects, singing birds and the hum of a lawnmower a few gardens away.

Daffodils, tulips and primroses are often the spring flowers that catch the eye, but there are also cheerful little forget-me-nots, flowering with abandon in a sunny border, while dainty lungwort with its spotted leaves and flowers the colours of boiled sweets brightens up a shady corner.

So many of the best flowering trees are spring bloomers too; magnolias, apple trees and flowering cherries are just a few. These glorious trees provide welcome food for pollinators and birds as well as a brilliant show in the garden. For a late spring spectacle, I wouldn't be without a handful of elegant alliums in the border, flowering from mid spring to early summer and marking that transition from spring into summer.

Daffodil

Cheery trumpeters of spring

Everyone recognizes the yellow trumpets of daffodils, but there is more variety to this group of bulbs than you might expect. Besides the bright and breezy classic yellow trumpets, there are tiny dwarf varieties, sometimes scented, those with pink or white trumpets and petals, and some with barely a trumpet at all.

- **Latin name:** *Narcissus* species and varieties
- **Plant type:** Bulb
- **Flower colour:** Yellow or white, sometimes with pink or orange trumpets
- **Flowering time:** February to May
- **Easy to grow:** Yes
- **Height:** 15–50cm (6–20in)
- **Hardy:** in USDA zones 3 to 9
- **Planting possibilities:** Beds and borders, naturalized in grass, woodland border, pots and containers
- **Growing conditions:** Full sun, part shade, well-drained soil
- **Wildlife value: 2**

GARDEN USE

A garden without daffodils would be very dull in spring. These easy-to-grow bulbs make a great show naturalized in a lawn or planted with other bulbs in borders, and the dwarf forms do wonders to brighten up a rock garden. Use them under later flowering shrubs such as roses to start the season with a splash of sunny colour, or plant them in single varieties in pots to make a spring display.

FAVOURITE DAFFODILS

'Tete a Tete' is the earliest and easiest to grow of all the dwarf daffodils. With its perfect miniature trumpet flowers and sunny yellow colour often appearing as early as February, it's an easy bulb to find space for, whether that's in a pot or in the border.

'Actea' is at the other end of the spectrum, with its pure white, fragrant flowers appearing in late April and May. I love the tall elegance of this variety in the border, with the rich orange-red, barely-there trumpets adding a colourful button to the centre of the flowers.

'Jetfire' is another dwarf form with bright yellow, swept-back petals and a brilliant orange trumpet. It grows to 25cm (10in) tall and flowers in March.

'Cheerfulness' has fragrant, double cream and white flowers and grows to 40cm (16in) tall in April. It's a lovely choice for cutting.

'Minnow' is the daintiest dwarf variety with perfect cream flowers with a tiny pale-yellow trumpet.

'February Gold' is a classic golden trumpet variety that is a reliable early bloomer and looks great naturalized in grass.

PLANTING PARTNERS

Taller *Narcissi* look good planted with other spring perennials, such as hellebores, as well as foliage plants like ferns and heucheras. They also work well with peonies and hardy geraniums that will grow to hide the fading foliage. Use the dwarf forms with other tiny bulbs, such as *Anemone blanda* and dwarf iris. Nearly all forms look good naturalized in lawns.

HOW TO GROW

Grow daffodils in beds and borders, making sure to plant the bulbs at the correct depth and to allow room for the bulbs to spread and multiply. They work well under shrubs and developing herbaceous plants that will hide the fading foliage, as it's vital that the bulbs fade naturally, with the nutrients sinking back into the bulb. Don't remove the yellowing leaves, however tempting it may be, as it will weaken these otherwise long-lived and robust bulbs.

PROPAGATION

Plant in September, in pots or directly into the ground. Plant the bulbs at three times their own depth in the ground, choosing a sunny or lightly shaded spot and well-drained soil.

WILDLIFE VALUE

Daffodils can attract pollinators, often when there are no other flowers around.

FASCINATING FACTS

The Romans brought daffodils to the UK, planting them in honour of fallen comrades and loved ones.

They also used the sap to treat wounds, which didn't work. In fact, it made the patient worse as the sap is a skin irritant, so take care when handling the bulbs. Daffodil bulbs were transported by sailing ships from Britain to the USA after the settlement of the Jamestown colony in 1609, often by women settlers who brought them along as a reminder of home.

Primrose

Brightens dull days

Latin name: *Primula vulgaris* and varieties

Plant type: Herbaceous perennial

Flower colour: All colours

Flowering time: February to April

Easy to grow: Yes

Height: 10–15cm (4–6in)

Hardy: in USDA zones 3 to 8

Planting possibilities: Beds and borders, woodland border, pots and containers

Growing conditions: Full sun, moist soil

Wildlife value: 4

GARDEN USE

The cheerful native primrose shines out in the dark days of late winter and early spring, and spreads through the garden if it's happy. The pale cream and yellow flowers of the native species look lovely in a woodland border under shrubs, while the bright bedding forms, which are best regarded as annuals, are good for pots and bedding schemes.

HOW TO GROW

Primroses love rich, moisture-retentive soil in dappled sun or partial shade. Those parts of the garden that stay moist throughout spring are ideal.

PROPAGATION

Sow seeds outside in winter, as a period of cold is needed to help the seeds germinate. Alternatively, look out for self-sown seedlings to transplant.

WILDLIFE VALUE

Primroses are an important nectar source for early-flying bees and other pollinators, while they also provide a food source for caterpillars.

FASCINATING FACTS

The name primrose derives from the Latin *prima* and *rosa*, meaning 'first rose', as it's often the first flower to appear in spring.

Columbine

Nodding, bonnet-like blooms

Latin name: *Aquilegia vulgaris* and varieties

Plant type: Herbaceous perennial

Flower colour: All colours

Flowering time: May and June

Easy to Grow: Yes

Height: 15–90cm (6–35in)

Hardy: in USDA zones 3 to 9

Planting possibilities: Beds and borders, cottage garden, cutting garden

Growing conditions: Full sun, moist soil

Wildlife value: 4

GARDEN USE

These charming nodding flowers look dainty and delicate, but they're actually tough and resilient, coping well with most garden situations. With its cottage garden looks, columbine lends itself to loose, informal plantings where they often self-seed freely. They look good with blousy shrubs such as roses and with grasses. Look out for the colourful 'Mrs Scott-Elliott' hybrids or 'William Guinness', with dramatic purple and white flowers.

HOW TO GROW

Columbines love a sunny or semi-shaded spot, as long as the soil doesn't dry out in summer.

PROPAGATION

Sow seeds in spring or summer, although they will often self-seed happily, to the point where they can become something of a nuisance. In that case, collect seed from some and deadhead the rest to prevent them from setting seed.

WILDLIFE VALUE

Attractive to bees, especially the long-tongued species, as well as some butterflies, hawk moths and hummingbirds.

FASCINATING FACTS

Strangely, this plant is named after two very different birds: the eagle and the dove. The Latin word for eagle, *aquila*, is the origin of the columbine's Latin name, *Aquilegia vulgaris*, as the flower resembles the claws of an eagle, while the Latin for dove, *columba*, describes the flowers looking like a cluster of doves and gives rise to the common name.

Peony

Blousy and beautiful

Latin name: *Paeonia*

Plant type: Herbaceous perennial

Flower colour: Crimson, pink, white or yellow

Flowering time: May and June

Easy to grow: Yes, but slow to establish

Height: 50cm–2m (20in–6½ft)

Hardy: in USDA zones 3 to 8

Planting possibilities: Beds and borders

Growing conditions: Full sun, good, well-drained soil

Wildlife value: 3

GARDEN USE

Peonies might be slow to establish, but they are tremendously rewarding as they will flower year after year, reliably producing huge bowl-shaped flowers in late spring and early summer. They look great in a traditional cottage garden planting but also blend well with more modern elements like grasses and alliums. Herbaceous peonies are the easiest to grow, the shrubby tree forms being prone to damage from cold winds and late frosts.

My favourite herbaceous varieties include the vigorous 'Buckeye Belle' with deep red flowers that contrast with the yellow stamens; 'Coral Charm' with glowing semi-double flowers; and 'Clair de Lune' or 'Moonlight' with soft yellow single flowers centred with golden stamens. The hardiest tree peony is *Paeonia lutea*, which produces a good show of single yellow flowers.

HOW TO GROW

Peonies prefer a sunny spot that is sheltered from the wind, so avoid shade and soil that is waterlogged or wet. They do not like being moved, so make sure to plant them where you will be happy to leave them undisturbed for years.

PROPAGATION

Grow from seed sown when ripe in autumn, although bear in mind that the resulting plants will not be true to form. Alternatively, divide and replant, making sure that each piece of the crown has roots and dormant buds.

WILDLIFE VALUE

Bees, butterflies and hoverflies are drawn to the large flowers if they are single or semi-double forms. Birds and mice will eat the large, shiny black seeds later in the autumn.

FASCINATING FACTS

Peonies can live to be more than a hundred years old.

Tulip

Elegant, richly coloured goblets

Tulips are surely the most elegant and lovely of all the spring flowers, with their soft pastel or richly coloured satin petals. Tulips come in all shapes and sizes, including the goblet-shaped classic forms, the delicately fringed varieties, and the wildly exotic parrot types. While each flower is a work of art in its own right, a mass of tulips makes a breathtaking show of colour in spring.

- **Latin name:** *Tulipa* species and varieties
- **Plant type:** Bulb
- **Flower colour:** All colours, except true blue
- **Flowering time:** March to May
- **Easy to grow:** Yes
- **Height:** 10–70cm (4–28in)
- **Hardy:** in USDA zones 3 to 7
- **Planting possibilities:** Beds and borders, cutting garden, pots and containers
- **Growing conditions:** Full sun, well-drained soil
- **Wildlife value: 3**

GARDEN USE

A handful of tulips brightens the spring garden no end, with even a few flowers making an elegant and colourful impact. Some varieties start flowering as early as March, while others go on until May, doing wonders for brightening your beds and borders, although they also look magnificently statuesque in pots and containers. With their long flowering period, tulips offer an invaluable transition from spring into summer.

FAVOURITE TULIPS

'Angelique' is a beauty. It's more peony than tulip with its ruffled double petals coloured a charming apple-blossom pink and white.

'Ballerina' is one of those unforgettable tulips with elegant, burnt orange, lily-like flowers on slender stems up to 60cm (24in) tall.

'Spring Green' has wonderfully striped petals in soft cream and green and looks great in a pot.

'Menton' is tall, growing up to 70cm (28in), with elegant, goblet-shaped flowers in a salmon-pink that look as if they're lit from within.

'Princess Irene' has early, delicately shaded purple and orange flowers in a classic goblet shape. They reach only 35cm (14in) tall, which is useful for pots and the front of a border.

Tulipa tarda is a species tulip with starry yellow flowers on short stems, which is great for naturalizing. It's also incredibly easy to grow and starts flowering early in March.

PLANTING PARTNERS

Tulips go well with almost any other plant. Dot taller varieties with herbaceous plants in the border, while shorter ones and species varieties add colour to a rock garden or gravel planting. I love the bold oranges and reds with lime greens, like *Euphorbia*, which set off the colours beautifully, while the softer pastel shades go well with silvery foliage plants like lamb's ear and lavender. For a show on the patio, plant them in a single variety in pots or layer with other spring bulbs for a season-long display in a single container.

HOW TO GROW

Tulips need fertile and well-drained soil, as the bulbs will tend to rot on clay, heavy soil. Grow them in full sun, where the conditions are moist in spring and warm and dry in summer, when the bulbs are dormant in the ground. Tulips grow brilliantly in pots, provided the container is a good size and the bulbs are not touching one another.

PROPAGATION

Plant in November, in pots or directly into the ground. Plant the bulbs at three times their depth in the ground, choosing a sunny and well-drained soil. Add a little grit to the planting hole if you're concerned your soil may be too damp.

WILDLIFE VALUE

Single-flowered varieties and species are good for pollinators such as bees, especially bumblebees.

FASCINATING FACTS

There are over 3,000 varieties of tulips, with more being bred every year. Some tulips are more sought after than others, and this passion led to Tulip Mania, a financial bubble that took place in Holland in the 1630s when some varieties were sold for more than the price of a house.

Allium

Majestic drumstick globes

Latin name: *Allium*

Plant type: Bulb

Flower colour: Purple, white or yellow

Flowering time: April to June

Easy to grow: Yes

Height: 50cm–2m (20in–6½ft)

Hardy: in USDA zones 3 to 8

Planting possibilities: Beds and borders

Growing conditions: Full sun, good, well-drained soil

Wildlife value: 4

GARDEN USE

Alliums make a great addition to the garden, whether they are the smaller varieties like chives edging a path, or the huge drumsticks rising out of herbaceous plants, adding substance and vibrant colour to otherwise soft and blousy planting. Plant them with hardy geraniums, peonies, roses and grasses, but they partner well with almost any other sun-loving plant. I like them with wafty grasses like *Stipa tenuissima*, and *Euphorbias*. There are so many glorious alliums that it's difficult to pick just a few. My top choices are always 'Gladiator' for its large purple flowers on stems over 1m (3f) tall; *Allium christophii* with starry globes some 20cm (8in) across; and chives, which are pretty, edible and a great plant for pollinators.

HOW TO GROW

Alliums are easy to plant and grow, provided they have the right conditions These bulbs need soil that is free-draining and not waterlogged and a spot that gets plenty of sunshine, as they will not flower well in shade.

PROPAGATION

Many alliums produce smaller offset bulbs that can be lifted and replanted or potted up. Alternatively, grow from seed sown when ripe in autumn, although bear in mind that the resulting plants will not be true to form and they will take some time to get to flowering size.

WILDLIFE VALUE

Bees, including honeybees and bumblebees, and butterflies and moths, are especially drawn to the large flowerheads.

FASCINATING FACTS

Alliums are some of the oldest cultivated edible plants, with the Romans credited with spreading edible alliums, such as garlic, throughout their empire. The flowers also feature in ancient Egyptian tombs, where they were regarded as symbols of the universe.

Wisteria

Elegant, fragrant cascades

Latin name: *Wisteria*

Plant type: Climber

Flower colour: Purple, blue, white or pink

Flowering time: April to June

Easy to grow: Yes

Height: 12m (39ft) or more

Hardy: in USDA zones 5 to 9

Planting possibilities: Walls, pergolas and arches

Growing conditions: Full sun, good, well-drained soil

Wildlife value: 4

GARDEN USE

Wisteria are large-growing and incredibly long-lived climbers, so picking the right spot is essential. They look fantastic clothing a sunny wall or trained over a pergola to offer leafy shade in summer. Grow them through trees, although they can become rather unruly, or you can train them into an umbrella-like standard, but to my mind they look their best on a wall or pergola, where the hanging, fragrant flowers can be fully appreciated. My favourite wisteria is the Chinese *Wisteria sinensis*, with wonderfully fragrant flowers appearing before the leaves in mid-April. Good forms include 'Prolific' with violet-blue flowers, and 'Amethyst' with fragrant, soft purple flowers. The Japanese species *Wisteria floribunda* flowers later in the season along with the leaves.

HOW TO GROW

Wisteria is vigorous and strong growing, needing a sturdy framework to train it against a wall or over a pergola or arch. Well-drained soil and a sunny spot are vital to produce the best flowers, as is a strict regime of pruning twice a year in August and February.

PROPAGATION

The easiest way to propagate wisteria is by layering in summer, or by taking softwood cuttings.

WILDLIFE VALUE

Wisteria is a magnet for bees of many species. It also provides cover and an invaluable habitat for small birds.

FASCINATING FACTS

The two main species of wisteria twine in different directions. Chinese wisteria twines in an anticlockwise direction, while Japanese wisteria twists clockwise. The Sierra Madre wisteria in California, which was planted in 1894, is the largest flowering plant in the world, covering over 4,000 square metres (1 acre) and weighing 250 tonnes (275 US tons).

Magnolia

Spectacular flowers on bare branches

Latin name: *Magnolia*

Plant type: Large shrub or tree

Flower colour: White or pink, occasionally yellow

Flowering time: March and April

Easy to grow: Moderately

Height: 2–20m (6½–66ft)

Hardy: in USDA zones 4 to 9

Planting possibilities: Specimen tree, woodland setting

Growing conditions: Sheltered spot, full sun or light shade, fertile, well-drained soil

Wildlife value: 2

GARDEN USE

Magnolias can become absolutely huge, so choose your variety carefully. The shrubby, starry varieties are great for small gardens and are easy to grow, while some of the larger tree types are more particular, requiring acidic soil to thrive. If it's a tree you're after, look at the *Magnolia x soulangeana* varieties, which will grow to around 6m (20ft) tall. I especially like 'Brozzonii' with creamy-white flowers, and 'Lennei' with rich pink-purple globe-like flowers. My pick of the shrubby, starry magnolias is *Magnolia x loebneri* 'Leonard Messel' with fragrant, soft pink flowers studding the bare branches even when it's very small.

HOW TO GROW

Magnolias can be a little tricky, needing a sheltered spot so their early flowers are protected from frost and cold winds, as well as rich, fertile soil. They often take a while to settle in, and a top dress of leaf mould or compost in spring helps the plants to establish.

PROPAGATION

Sow seeds in autumn, once they're ripe, although be warned that germination can take a year or more. Take heel cuttings in summer, although again allow plenty of time for rooting to take place.

WILDLIFE VALUE

Magnolia trees provide roosting habitats for birds, while some bird species in the USA also eat the seeds, and beetles will visit the flowers.

Magnolias are some of the most ancient flowering plants and are found in fossils dating back over 100 million years. They actually existed before bees, so they are pollinated by beetles, producing masses of pollen rather than nectar.

FASCINATING FACTS

A pair of southern magnol as are believed to have once been the cldest trees growing in the grounds of the White House in Washington DC before one was cut down. They were planted between 1829 and 1837 by President Andrew Jackson in memory of his wife, Rachel, who died two weeks after he won the election.

Wallflower

Scented stalwarts of spring

Wallflowers, especially the spring-flowering *Erysimum cheiri*, have been somewhat out of fashion, yet, to my mind, their flower power, ease of growing and wonderful scent make them a brilliant addition to any garden. Regarded as biennial, these are actually short-lived perennials, which means, in milder winters, they'll go on flowering year after year until they get too woody and ungainly to keep. Perennial forms flower into the summer but often lack the scent of the early varieties.

Latin name: *Erysimum* species and varieties

Plant type: Herbaceous perennial

Flower colour: Cream, yellow, orange, red, pink, crimson and purple

Flowering time: March to August

Easy to grow: Yes

Height: 15–50cm (6–20in)

Hardy: in USDA zones 3 to 9

Planting possibilities: Beds and borders, pots and containers, wildlife garden, cottage garden

Growing conditions: Full sun, any soil

Wildlife value: 3

GARDEN USE

As well as being incredibly easy to grow and hugely forgiving of soil and site, wallflowers provide great blooms and a fabulous scent for very little effort. With their wide range of colours, they blend well with many other plants and make for a good springtime filler in the border or in pots.

FAVOURITE WALLFLOWERS

'Vulcan' has rich, deep red flowers with purple tones and has a wonderful scent that is characteristic of one of the shorter-lived *Erysimum cheiri* varieties.

'Fire King' is another *Erysimum cheiri* variety with a fantastic scent and glowing, flaming flowers.

'Sunset Purple', also an *Erysimum cheiri* form, with beautiful faded purple petals and a good scent.

'Bowles Mauve' is the classic long-flowering perennial form with grey-green foliage and tonal mauve and purple flower spikes.

'Red Jep' is a perennial form with red and purple flowers and a good scent, which is uncommon in these perennial types.

PLANTING PARTNERS

Wallflowers look great in the border, adding a splash of spring colour to the front or dotted among spring-flowering bulbs. They look great with daffodils and tulips and will combine well with them in pots and containers, as well as in the ground. Use the perennial forms in the border, where they will add colour and structure for a long season.

HOW TO GROW

Wallflowers of all types are incredibly forgiving of soil, growing in the poorest conditions and even springing up out of cracks in walls, hence their name. But they do need sunshine – and plenty of it – to flower at their best so avoid any but the lightest shade if at all possible.

PROPAGATION

Take semi-ripe cuttings of perennial forms in summer and they will root readily. Sow seed of the short-lived varieties in spring, setting out the plants in autumn or the following spring. These will often self-seed happily if left to their own devices.

WILDLIFE VALUE

These are great plants for pollinators, with the scented forms attracting bees and the perennial forms providing a long season of pollen-rich flowers.

FASCINATING FACTS

As the name suggests, wallflowers grow very readily in walls, and the seeds of the first wallflowers were believed to have arrived in the UK with a shipment of stone. After his invasion of 1066, William the Conqueror imported stone from Caen, northern France, to build his castles, and it's believed that wallflower seeds were among these stones.

The classic garden wallflower was a popular favourite in North American gardens by the beginning of the 18th century. But the many species of *Erysimum* have a wide global range, with native species found in temperate Eurasia, North Africa and Macaronesia, and from North America to parts of Central America including Costa Rica. Many wallflowers are very specific to small areas, such as *E.etnense*, which is local to Mount Etna, and *E.franciscanum*, found on the north Californian coast.

Forsythia

A cloud of yellow in spring

- **Latin name:** *Forsythia*
- **Plant type:** Shrub
- **Flower colour:** Yellow
- **Flowering time:** March and April
- **Easy to grow:** Yes
- **Height:** 60cm–2m (2–6½ft)
- **Hardy:** in USDA zones 4 to 9
- **Planting possibilities:** Beds and borders, hedges, cutting garden
- **Growing conditions:** Full sun or light shade, well-drained soil
- **Wildlife value: 3**

GARDEN USE

Forsythia makes a good background shrub in the border, where its green foliage sets off herbaceous plants, such as Michaelmas daisies, wonderfully in summer. But it has its moment of sunshine glory in the spring when few other shrubs are flowering. The bare branches are covered in bright yellow flowers that combine especially well in the border with daffodils. It's a good plant for pruning and shaping and makes a great hedge, or even a spectacular arch.

HOW TO GROW

Forsythia is a very forgiving and easy-to-grow shrub, happy in most soils but flowering at its best in a sunny spot. Prune in late spring or early summer, once the flowers have faded and the leaves appear.

PROPAGATION

Take cuttings in October from strong shoots of new growth, rooting them in a nursery bed outdoors. Alternatively, layer branches in October, weighing or pegging them down. Both cuttings and layers will take a year to settle and root properly.

WILDLIFE VALUE

These twiggy shrubs provide good shelter for birds, and some will feed on the flower buds. The flowers themselves are believed to offer a little nectar and pollen for pollinators, though bees are often attracted to them.

FASCINATING FACTS

When it rains, forsythia flowers tip downwards to protect their pollen. Although they may seem to have little in common, forsythia is related to the olive tree.

Flowering cherry

Classic spring blossoms

A cherry blossom tree in full flower is a wonder of the springtime. There are so many varieties, shapes and sizes to choose from that there is one to suit every garden, large or small. The sugared almond shades of the pink and white blossoms look magical against a blue sky, and when the cherries are in flower, there's a feeling that summer is on its way.

- **Latin name:** *Prunus* species and varieties
- **Plant type:** Tree
- **Flower colour:** White or pink
- **Flowering time:** March to May
- **Easy to grow:** Yes
- **Height:** 2–12m (6½–39ft)
- **Hardy:** in USDA zones 5 to 8
- **Planting possibilities:** Specimen tree, border planting, smaller varieties in pots and containers
- **Growing conditions:** Full sun, part shade, well-drained soil
- **Wildlife value: 3**

GARDEN USE

A flowering cherry tree makes a great addition to any garden, providing beautiful blossoms in the spring, a good habitat for birds in summer, and beautiful leaf colour in autumn. Plant smaller varieties in pots, while taller forms look great in the border underplanted with spring-flowering plants and bulbs. A single-specimen cherry planted on its own in the lawn also makes a wonderful sight.

FAVOURITE FLOWERING CHERRIES

'Accolade' produces masses of soft pink, semi-double flowers in April, followed by brilliant leaf colour in autumn. It's a good choice for a medium-sized garden, growing to 8m (26ft) tall.

'Kojo-no-mai' is a brilliant variety for growing in a pot, with tiny white flowers, a compact habit and lovely autumn colour.

'Shogetsu' is a personal favourite for its spreading habit and beautiful, soft pink double blossoms in late April and early May. It grows up to 8m (26ft) but is often shorter due to its spreading habit.

'Pink Shell' is a good choice for smaller spaces, with dainty, single shell-pink flowers and an elegant habit up to 4m (13ft) tall.

'Tai Haku' is not for the smaller garden but is a magnificent choice of cherry tree. It's known as the great white cherry for its big, robust habit, up to 12m (39ft) or so in height, and its beautiful, huge, single white flowers late in the season.

'Amanogawa' is known as the flagpole cherry, as it has a very upright, columnar habit, which is useful for a smaller garden or for planting in a border. It grows to 6m (20ft) or so tall, with semi-double pale pink blossoms late in the season.

PLANTING PARTNERS

Flowering cherries look wonderful underplanted with spring flowers such as daffodils, tulips, lungwort and primroses. In summer, when their shade is dense, underplant them with ferns, hostas and other shade-loving varieties.

HOW TO GROW

Pick a sheltered spot for your cherry tree to protect the delicate blossoms from wind and cold. They need a fertile soil that is well drained, and a sunny or lightly shaded spot. Cherries are shallow rooting, so they make a good choice for planting near buildings.

PROPAGATION

Most named varieties are best grown by grafting, which is most successful when done professionally.

WILDLIFE VALUE

These trees make great roosts for birds, some of which will eat the blossoms, and the single and semi-double flowered varieties are also good for pollinators, including many types of bees.

FASCINATING FACTS

In Japanese culture, going to see the cherry blossom, or *hanami*, is a big event where thousands of people travel to witness the great spectacle. The blossoms, or *sakura*, symbolize the fleeting nature of life, but they also represent renewal and happiness.

Lungwort

Spotted leaves and sweet flowers

Latin name: *Pulmonaria*

Plant type: Herbaceous perennial

Flower colour: Blue, pink or white

Flowering time: March and April

Easy to grow: Yes

Height: 30cm (12in)

Hardy: in USDA zones 4 to 9

Planting possibilities: Beds and borders, woodland garden, shady spots

Growing conditions: Light or full shade, well-drained but damp soil

Wildlife value: 4

GARDEN USE

Lungwort is a little unsung hero of the spring garden, producing masses of small flowers freely over a long season. As well as their lovely bell flowers in shades of blue, pink, white, or two-tone blue and pink, the leaves are beautifully spotted and striped, adding foliage interest and brightness to shady corners. Plant them with ferns and hellebores, and choose from various forms, including 'Leopard' with strongly spotted leaves and pink flowers, 'Majeste' with almost entirely silver leaves, and 'Opal' with luminous pale blue flowers.

HOW TO GROW

Lungwort needs shade more than anything else, although moisture-retentive soil is also beneficial, so avoid soil that dries out completely. Water well in dry spells, and top dress with garden compost or leaf mould every spring

PROPAGATION

Divide and replant in early autumn or spring.

WILDLIFE VALUE

Don't be fooled, as despite their small size, these little flowers are packed with pollen and nectar, attracting bees and other pollinators.

FASCINATING FACTS

Lungwort was believed to be beneficial for lung complaints, which gave rise to both its common and Latin names.

Lilac

Fragrant flowering tree

Latin name: *Syringa vulgaris* and varieties

Plant type: Tree or shrub

Flower colour: Purple, mauve, pink, red or white

Flowering time: April to June

Easy to grow: Yes

Height: 4–8m (13–26ft)

Hardy: in USDA zones 3 to 7

Planting possibilities: Beds and borders, cottage garden, cutting garden

Growing conditions: Full sun, tolerant of most soils except acidic

Wildlife value: 3

GARDEN USE

The scent of lilacs is a joy in late spring and they're reliable, offering wonderfully fragrant heads of flowers. Plant a lilac in the back of a border, alone, in a group, or close to a path, where you can appreciate the scent. My favourites are 'Primrose' with creamy flowers, 'Madame Lemoine' which is pure white, and the rather cumbersomely named 'Andenken an Ludwig Späth', which has rich wine-red flowers.

HOW TO GROW

Lilacs are easy to grow in most garden soils and situations, and they love a sunny spot. The only drawback is they tend to sucker a great deal, becoming a thicket of stems if left unmanaged. Prune after flowering to maintain a single or multi-stem trunk, and don't be afraid to prune hard if necessary, as they will tolerate this.

PROPAGATION

Take softwood cuttings in summer or remove a sucker with some root attached.

WILDLIFE VALUE

Lilac flowers are nectar-rich and there are plenty of them, which makes them very popular with long-tongued bees, butterflies and moths. They also provide good shelter and roosts for birds in summer.

FASCINATING FACTS

Related to the olive tree, lilac wood is just as useful for carving and the wood is beautifully coloured in cream, brown and purple. It's dense but easy to work with, and is used to make musical instruments, knife handles, pens and bowls.

Forget-me-not

Cottage garden cute

Latin name: *Myosotis* species and varieties

Plant type: Annual or herbaceous perennial

Flower colour: Blue, pink or white

Flowering time: April to June

Easy to grow: Yes

Height: 15–25cm (6–10in)

Hardy: in USDA zones 3 to 9

Planting possibilities: Beds and borders, cottage garden, woodland border

Growing conditions: Full sun, light shade, moist soil

Wildlife value: 3

GARDEN USE

Forget-me-nots make a great ground cover in spring, providing a carpet of sky-blue flowers beneath foliage plants like hostas and ferns. They look great under trees and shrubs and alongside a path, and combine especially well with other spring flowers such as tulips and wallflowers.

HOW TO GROW

These small plants thrive in damp, woodland-edge conditions, although they can also cope with full sun, as long as the soil is enriched with organic matter. They're often best treated as annuals, removing the plants after flowering as they become scruffy and spotted with mildew.

PROPAGATION

Sow seeds in late spring or summer, although they will often self-seed happily, to the point where they can become something of a nuisance. To prevent this, deadhead and cut back hard once the main flowering has finished.

WILDLIFE VALUE

These little flowers are very attractive to bees, while the seeds are great for small birds.

FASCINATING FACTS

In Newfoundland and Labrador in Canada, forget-me-nots are worn as symbols of remembrance, much like poppies in the UK and USA.

What to do in the garden during spring

With everything growing but still the odd frost to watch out for, there's a lot to do in the garden at this time of year. This is prime time for sowing both indoors and outside, whether it's vegetables, herbs or flowers, as the soil is warming nicely, even if the air temperature still feels a bit chilly. Start sweet peas and half-hardy annuals off indoors in March, while the tougher hardy annuals can be sown outdoors in April. It's a good time for planting out, too, with the April showers set to water new plants in nicely, and the perfect time to divide many herbaceous perennials, such as Michaelmas daisies. Make the most of the milder weather by getting on with pruning before plants sprout too much. Woody herbaceous plants like penstemons can be cut back hard to new shoots, while lavender will benefit from a good trim to stop it getting straggly. Don't get too carried away by the promise of a few warm, summer-like days, though – the frosts and cold nights aren't over yet. To be on the safe side, it's wise to wait until the end of May before planting out all those tender little lovelies like *Pelargonium* and cosmos that you've been carefully nurturing through the spring.

- The warm spring days will lead to an explosion of weeds, and it's a good idea to keep clearing them now before they set seed and make the problem worse. The warm, moist soil will make it easy to pull them out, roots and all. Finish off with a nice top dress of garden compost to help suppress any newly germinating weeds.

- Prune shrub roses, removing dead, diseased or damaged wood first. After that, prune back to an outward-facing bud, aiming for an open goblet shape to allow for good airflow, which will keep the plant healthy and the new blooms in good condition.

- Snowdrops settle in far better when planted 'in the green', just after they have finished flowering. Early spring is the perfect time to lift and split clumps of snowdrops and winter aconites. Simply lift a clump gently with a trowel, split it into smaller sections, and replant the bulbs carefully at the same height elsewhere in the garden.

- Cut back grasses and herbaceous perennials that were left over winter to add interest and provide habitats for wildlife. Cut back herbaceous plants to the crown, taking care not to damage the new shoots that will already be developing. Evergreen grasses such as stipa can be given a 'haircut', trimming off the dead material lightly, allowing the new shoots to develop.

- Get your stakes in place for any tall-growing plants now, so that the plants grow through them naturally. Plants like Michaelmas daisies, delphiniums and dahlias all need some support, whether that's a frame, a shrub or a handful of canes and string. Place canes or supports, crisscrossed with string, and the plant's foliage will hide the structure as they grow.

- Deadhead daffodils and tulips as they finish flowering to prevent the seedpods from swelling, as that will take energy away from the bulb. Don't be tempted to remove the tired and yellowing foliage, though. While you're deadheading, tidy up any spent blooms, such as pansies, violas and primroses, as this will keep them reflowering.

Summer

After the fickle days of spring, the milder summer weather is a joy for gardeners and plants alike. Admittedly, weeds and pests also thrive in these balmy conditions, but that's where I hope that my ecologically balanced garden comes into its own.

Increased wildlife, whether nuisance pests or welcome pollinators, also attracts natural predators like birds that will keep any problems at a more manageable level. Allowing a certain amount of self-seeding of annuals, and planting herbaceous plants, covers the ground, reducing space for weeds to establish, and helping to retain moisture close to the soil, a boon in dry spells.

In my garden, the start of summer is all about early bloomers: blousy peonies, statuesque foxgloves and ethereal roses, with an understorey of flowering plants like hardy geraniums. Overhead, the branches of the flowering cherry are leafy and dense, offering shade on hot days. Irises have their moment in the sun, their velvet flowers contrasting with sharp leaves and, for a brief spell, the garden is fragrant with the flowers of mock orange. In any gaps I plant salvias, which flower through the season, complemented later by dusky lavender.

High summer is for annuals: poppies, cornflowers and sunflowers, to name but a few. I could create a whole rainbow garden with these, and they will self-seed happily if left to their own devices. Another self-seeder I let run free is *Verbena bonariensis*, a beauty that attracts pollinators to its potent flowers. It will flower from midsummer into autumn, alongside snapdragons and dahlias, until the shorter, damper days arrive, signalling the end of summer.

Rose

Classic summer flowers

Few flowers make a garden more complete than a rose. Their blousy blooms in beautiful colours paint the garden at its peak, blending with perennials, shrubs and grasses seamlessly. Whether it's shrub roses in the border, climbing roses trained on walls or obelisks, or rambling roses clambering into trees, these versatile plants offer a huge variety of sizes, shapes and flower colours, as well as great value for wildlife.

Latin name: *Rosa* species and varieties

Plant type: Shrub or climber

Flower colour: Red, crimson, pink, yellow, buff and white and variations, including some striped varieties

Flowering time: Main season is June, with some varieties continuing into autumn

Easy to grow: Yes, although care and attention is needed

Height: 30cm–1.5m (12in–5ft) for shrubs, climbers and ramblers from 2.5–18m (8–69ft)

Hardy: in USDA zones 5 to 9

Planting possibilities: Beds, border, arches and smaller varieties in containers

Growing conditions: Full sun, good soil

Wildlife value: 4

GARDEN USE

Roses come in all sizes, from tiny patio types to huge ramblers that will happily make themselves at home in a tree. Roses are incredibly useful garden plants, working equally effectively in a formal design as in a naturalistic planting, but perhaps their most common use is in a mixed border, adding structure, height and many, many flowers to a summer show.

FAVOURITE ROSES

'Cecile Brunner' is a strong climber that produces masses of small, perfectly furled pale pink flowers in June and July, and again in September.

'Kew Gardens' produces plenty of single white flowers centred with yellow stamens throughout the season. It's a brilliant shrub for health, vigour and attracting pollinators, and it looks lovely in a natural-style planting.

'Olivia Rose Austin' is one I return to time after time for its blousy pink flowers, repeated steadily throughout the summer, its strong growth, and its superb tolerance for poorer soils and conditions.

***Rosa moyesii* 'Geranium'** has brilliant pink-red single flowers with golden anthers on strong stems, which are good for pollinating insects, followed by large, shiny red, flask-shaped hips in autumn.

'Charles de Mills' is an old variety of rose with rich purple, densely petalled flowers and a lovely scent. It's a strong, stately plant and is very resilient to weather and disease.

'Paul's Himalayan Musk' is a personal favourite with its clusters of tiny pale pink flowers in June. While the flowers may be small, there are lots of them, and the plant itself is huge, happily taking over a tree where the blossom cascades down for a few weeks of wonder every summer.

PLANTING PARTNERS

There is a rose for almost every garden style, ranging from patio pot varieties for bedding schemes to formal rose garden varieties for planting on their own. Old roses summon up the glory days of yesteryear with their evocative colours and fragrance and work well towards the back of a mixed border, where they add structure. Climbers are useful for clothing walls and fences, while wild-growing ramblers will run amok through an old tree or over a shed roof. Some shrub varieties have huge, blousy flowers that look perfectly at home in a cottage garden, while the simple, single-flowered forms go well in more naturalistic planting schemes. Plant them with grasses for a modern look or use shrub roses as an informal flowering hedge to divide the garden.

HOW TO GROW

Roses need a sunny spot with rich, moist soil that is regularly topped up with an organic mulch of well-rotted garden compost or manure. Some varieties will cope with poorer conditions, although they won't tolerate waterlogged soil. Pruning shrubs and climbers every year is essential, both to manage their growth and shape and to promote flowering.

PROPAGATION

Take softwood cuttings of new growth in late spring or summer, or firmer wood cuttings in late summer when the stems are riper and more mature.

WILDLIFE VALUE

Single and semi-double forms of roses provide an important late-season source of food for bees, flies, butterflies and beetles. All roses offer woody cover for small birds, which often hop about picking off insects. Small birds also appreciate the shelter that rambling and climbing roses give them.

FASCINATING FACTS

The oldest documented living rose is a wild dog rose, *Rosa canina*, that is believed to be a thousand years old and grows on the wall of St Mary's Cathedral in Hildesheim, Germany. Despite the cathedral being bombed in 1945, the rose survived and regrew from its roots.

Poppy

Delicate, tissue-paper petals

Latin name: *Papaver*

Plant type: Annual or herbaceous perennial

Flower colour: Red, pink, orange, yellow or white

Flowering time: May to September, depending on species and sowing time

Easy to grow: Yes, very

Height: 30–90cm (12–35in)

Hardy: in USDA zones 3 to 9

Planting possibilities: Beds and borders

Growing conditions: Full sun, any soil

Wildlife value: 4

GARDEN USE

There is a choice of poppies that work well in gardens. The perennial oriental poppy is great for a sunny mixed border, where it can establish and bulk up. Favourites include the silky mauve 'Patty's Plum' and the classic scarlet 'Beauty of Livermere'. Fast-growing annual forms like the field poppy and the opium poppy are great fun to grow, with the opium poppies also producing fantastic seed heads for drying. Easy to grow, these make great additions to annual schemes and fillers for odd gaps in borders. Look out for the lovely 'Ladybird' with scarlet petals spotted with black at the base, 'Shirley Mix' with brilliant red and pastel shades, and 'Lauren's Grape' with large, single, rich purple flowers.

HOW TO GROW

Poppies, both perennial and annual, need a well-drained, sunny spot to thrive. Annual forms are best sown where they are to flower, as they will not transplant readily.

PROPAGATION

Sow seeds in spring or in September to flower the following season. Divide and replant the roots of perennial forms in March and April.

WILDLIFE VALUE

Bees, butterflies and hoverflies are drawn to the readily available pollen dusting the stamens, while birds and mice love the plentiful seeds.

FASCINATING FACTS

After World War One, the poppy came to represent memorial and remembrance. The paper poppy is worn on Remembrance Day, 11th November, in the UK and many other countries. This simple poppy was designed to be put together with just one hand because the first factory, established in the UK in 1922, employed disabled veterans on the production line. It continues to do so and produces about 36 million poppies annually.

The final Monday in May, Memorial Day, is when poppies, often Buddy Poppies, are worn in the USA. Created in 1923, the Buddy Poppy was also designed to be assembled by disabled veterans, as it still is today.

Sunflower

Huge, sun-loving daisies

Latin name: *Helianthus*

Plant type: Annual or herbaceous perennial

Flower colour: Usually yellow or orange

Flowering time: July to September, depending on species and sowing time

Easy to grow: Yes, very

Height: 50cm–3m (20in–10ft)

Hardy: in USDA zones 6 to 9

Planting possibilities: Beds and borders, kitchen garden

Growing conditions: Full sun, any soil

Wildlife value: 5

GARDEN USE

Native to the USA, annual sunflowers are brilliant showpiece plants for the kitchen garden, in particular, where their bright colours and stature, as well as their ability to attract pollinating insects and birds, make them good companion plants to fruit and vegetables. Use them in annual plantings where their height makes a bold statement, or in 'hot' colour schemes of reds and oranges. Perennial varieties like the softly coloured 'Lemon Queen' make a statuesque addition to a perennial border. My favourite annual varieties include the elegant 'Claret' with lots of rich, red-brown flowers on branching stems up to 1.5m (5ft) tall, and 'Valentine' with soft yellow petals surrounding a deep brown centre. If you're competing with the neighbours, 'Russian Giant' is the hugely tall form with flowers the size of dinner plates.

HOW TO GROW

All sunflowers need a sunny spot, sheltered from the wind, which may break their stems, and soil that isn't waterlogged or wet. The taller varieties will need staking as they grow, and a good mulch of garden compost also helps.

PROPAGATION

Sow seeds in spring. Divide and replant the roots of perennial forms in March and April.

WILDLIFE VALUE

Bees, butterflies and hoverflies are drawn to the huge flowers and their pollen, while birds and mice love the plentiful seeds later in the autumn.

FASCINATING FACTS

Sunflowers have been cultivated for more than 4,500 years, undoubtedly because the whole plant is edible: flower head, seeds, leaves, stalks and roots. The seeds were milled to create flour, while the flower heads can be thickly sliced and fried, and the seeds and oil are still widely used in cooking.

Nasturtium

Bright, easy and edible

- **Latin name:** *Tropaeolum*
- **Plant type:** Annual
- **Flower colour:** Red, orange, yellow and cream
- **Flowering time:** June to October
- **Easy to grow:** Yes, very
- **Height:** 30cm–2m (12in–6½ft)
- **Hardy:** in USDA zones 3 to 10
- **Planting possibilities:** Beds and borders, kitchen garden, pots and containers
- **Growing conditions:** Full sun, well-drained soil
- **Wildlife value:** 4

GARDEN USE

Nasturtiums are incredibly useful plants, covering a huge area of ground in a single season, flowering madly, and requiring no effort whatsoever from the gardener. Plant them in the kitchen garden, where they will attract pollinators, as well as drawing white butterflies away from your cabbages. Alternatively, use the smaller varieties in pots and containers, while the climbing forms will quickly cover a trellis or obelisk, and a handful of nasturtiums will hide an unfinished area for the entire season. My favourite nasturtiums include the colourful 'Alaska' with marbled leaves and brilliantly coloured flowers, or the more elegant 'Empress of India' with rich crimson flowers, blue-green leaves, and a compact habit. A good climbing variety is 'Orange Troika' with marbled leaves setting off vivid orange flowers.

HOW TO GROW

Nasturtiums are incredibly easy to grow, thriving in poor but well-drained soil in a sunny location. However, if the soil is too rich, you'll end up with more leaves than flowers.

PROPAGATION

Grow from seed sown under cover in March, or outside from late March to May. These plants are so vigorous, you can happily sow the seeds directly where the plants are to grow or in pots to plant out later.

WILDLIFE VALUE

Nasturtiums are attractive to many pollinators, with long-tongued bees especially enjoying nectar from the flowers. As well as moths and other butterflies, large and small white butterflies are drawn to nasturtiums to lay their eggs, and their caterpillars feed on the leaves rather than on your cabbages.

FASCINATING FACTS

Nasturtiums were once known as Indian cress, as they were introduced to Europe from the Americas, then known as the Indies; they were eaten much like cress as a salad, which you can still do today as all parts of the plant are edible.

Lavender

Essential fragrance of summer

Latin name: *Lavandula*

Plant type: Shrub

Flower colour: Usually blue or purple, sometimes pink or white

Flowering time: July to September

Easy to grow: Yes

Height: 50cm–1.2m (20in–4ft)

Hardy: in USDA zones 5 to 10

Planting possibilities: Beds and borders, gravel garden

Growing conditions: Full sun, good, well-drained soil

Wildlife value: 5

GARDEN USE

Lavender is a classic plant for cottage gardens, lining a path or steps, where they look wonderful with roses, hardy geraniums and sun-loving annuals such as cornflowers and sweet peas. For a more modern look, plant lavender in a gravel garden with other plants that love good drainage, like verbena, salvia and grasses. French lavender, *Lavandula stoechas*, is a somewhat tender beauty for pots that needs shelter, but good, hardy varieties include 'Imperial Gem', which is perfect for hedges, and 'Hidcote', which is the classic English lavender, flowering for weeks on end and attracting every bee for miles around.

HOW TO GROW

All lavenders need a sunny spot, with the more tender ones also needing shelter from cold winds. The soil should be light and free-draining, and definitely not waterlogged or wet.

PROPAGATION

Take softwood cuttings in spring or 'heel' cuttings in summer from shoots that are not flowering.

WILDLIFE VALUE

Lavender is a magnet for bees, butterflies and hoverflies throughout its long flowering period, while afterwards the plentiful seeds attract birds and mice.

FASCINATING FACTS

While we tend to think of simply English and French types of lavender, both of which are actually from the Mediterranean, there are in fact 45 different species, originating from the Mediterranean, the Middle East and India, as well as more than 450 varieties. Lavender has a long history of use, with traces of the herb and a hint of its scent reported upon when Tutankhamun's tomb was opened in 1923.

Cornflower *or* bachelor's button

Flowers the colour of summer skies

Latin name: *Centaurea*

Plant type: Annual or herbaceous perennial

Flower colour: Usually blue, sometimes burgundy, pink or white

Flowering time: May to September

Easy to grow: Yes

Height: 45–75cm (17¾–29½in)

Hardy: in USDA zones 3 to 9

Planting possibilities: Beds and borders, cutting garden

Growing conditions: Full sun, any soil, preferably not too dry

Wildlife value: 4

GARDEN USE

Cornflowers, both perennial and annual, are an easy, attractive win for the gardener as they're so easy to grow and give a lot of flowers for little effort. Use the perennial forms in a mixed or herbaceous border, deadheading the flowers as they fade to keep them coming. Sow the annual varieties in a cut flower border, particularly to fill odd bare spots, or in an annual bed. Favourite varieties include the perennial 'Amethyst in Snow' with white petals and a purple centre, and the annual variety 'Black Ball' with rich burgundy flowers.

HOW TO GROW

While the annual varieties need a sunny spot, the perennial forms are tougher and more forgiving, tolerating partial shade without any problems. They're also very forgiving of soil, but they won't cope with drought conditions, and the annual forms especially need to be kept well-watered.

PROPAGATION

Divide perennial varieties in spring, and sow annual varieties where they are to grow in autumn or early spring.

WILDLIFE VALUE

Hoverflies and bees especially love cornflowers for their sweet pollen, while small birds love the seeds.

FASCINATING FACTS

The pollen of annual cornflowers is incredibly sweet, with a sugar content of 34 per cent. Each flower produces 0.2mg of sugar per day, which makes cornflowers much appreciated by both bees and their keepers.

Vervain *or* purple top

Airy, seemingly delicate flowers

Latin name: *Verbena bonariensis*

Plant type: Annual or herbaceous perennial

Flower colour: Purple

Flowering time: July to October

Easy to grow: Yes

Height: 1–2m (3–6½ft)

Hardy: in USDA zones 7 to 11

Planting possibilities: Beds and borders, gravel garden

Growing conditions: Full sun, well-drained soil

Wildlife value: 4

GARDEN USE

As well as several types of perennial, verbenas are also available as annuals for pots and bedding schemes, but *Verbena bonariensis* is by far the stateliest of them all, with its open 'bony' habit that is wonderfully see-through and works brilliantly with grasses. It's a plant for a loose, naturalistic planting, where its long flowering period keeps the show going with no effort from the gardener whatsoever.

HOW TO GROW

A sunny spot and well-drained soil are a must for verbena, and if it's happy, it will self-seed, which might become something of a nuisance. Plant it in a sheltered spot to prevent the tall stems becoming bent and broken. A dry mulch around the top of the plant will help the plant overwinter, if you're in a very cold area.

PROPAGATION

Simply allow verbenas to self-seed and move the resulting seedlings, or sow seed in autumn or early spring.

WILDLIFE VALUE

All pollinators love this plant; the flowers might be small, but they are hugely appealing to hoverflies, bees, butterflies and many moth species. Birds also appreciate the seeds.

FASCINATING FACTS

Native to South America, this plant has become somewhat invasive in parts of the USA and features on the watch lists for invasive plants for several southern US states.

Cranesbill *or* hardy geranium

Charming flowers and filigree foliage

For early summer flowers, look no further than cranesbills, or hardy geraniums, as they're often called. These little plants are tough, hardy, reliable and resistant to pests and diseases, flowering wonderfully in May and June and sometimes for longer, depending on the variety.

- **Latin name:** *Geranium* species and varieties
- **Plant type:** Herbaceous perennial
- **Flower colour:** Purple, pink, blue or white
- **Flowering time:** Main season is June, with some repeat flowering
- **Easy to grow:** Yes
- **Height:** 15–60cm (6–24in)
- **Hardy:** in USDA zones 3 to 9
- **Planting possibilities:** Beds and borders
- **Growing conditions:** Full sun, part shade, any soil except dry
- **Wildlife value:** 4

GARDEN USE

Cranesbills are the perfect garden plant. But it's their pretty flowers that make them the most popular garden plant in the UK, and in the top ten of favourite USA plants.

FAVOURITE CRANESBILLS

'Rozanne' has the longest flowering period of any cranesbill, with glowing blue blooms steadily produced from June to October. It needs some space to romp around, so it makes brilliant ground cover.

'Mrs Kendall Clark' has the most delicate, ice-blue veined flowers above mounds of finely cut, rich green leaves. Perfect for cottage gardens.

'Kashmir White' is long-flowering with finely cut foliage and large, veined white flowers. It's a little shorter than many varieties, reaching only 45cm (17¾in), which makes it useful for the front of a border.

'Ann Folkard' has rich magenta flowers, each centred with a black eye, contrasting wonderfully with the lime-green foliage.

Geranium phaeum **'Album'** is one of those useful plants that will tolerate shade, both damp and dry. Once it establishes, it forms a mound of purple splotched leaves topped by shining white nodding flowers in early summer.

PLANTING PARTNERS

Cranesbills go well with almost any garden plant, in my experience, partly because their flowers come en masse in a myriad of clear colours, but also because the textured foliage creates a mound of vibrant green even before the flowers appear. Plant taller varieties with cottage garden favourites such as roses, lavender and other herbaceous perennials as well as annuals. Use the dwarf forms in rock and gravel gardens, where their neat, mounded habit adds structure. In a more modern planting, the pastel shades blend well with grasses.

HOW TO GROW

Cranesbills are very forgiving; as long as the soil is moist and well-drained, they will cope with conditions ranging from full sun to full shade, depending on the variety. Mulch them annually with well-rotted garden compost or manure.

PROPAGATION

Look out for self-seeded seedlings springing up by themselves or divide pieces off the parent plant in spring.

WILDLIFE VALUE

With so many single flowers produced over such a long period, these plants provide plenty of nectar and pollen for pollinators right in the peak of the season. The seeds are much loved by birds, especially bullfinches.

FASCINATING FACTS

The cranesbill is a true geranium and is hardy, tough and a good all-round garden plant, not to be confused with the bedding geranium, which is truly a *Pelargonium* and is tender and mostly used for summer bedding displays in pots and containers.

Snapdragon

Spikes of fascinating flowers

Latin name: *Antirrhinum majus*

Plant type: Herbaceous perennial, but often grown as an annual

Flower colour: Any colour except blue

Flowering time: July to October

Easy to grow: Yes, more demanding to propagate

Height: 10cm–1.2m (4in–4ft)

Hardy: in USDA zones 7 to 10

Planting possibilities: Beds and borders, cutting garden

Growing conditions: Full sun, well-drained soil

Wildlife value: 3

GARDEN USE

With their 'snapping' flowers in a myriad of gorgeous colours, these are one of the first flowers I remember from childhood, and they still hold the same fascination. Plant the taller varieties in the border and cutting garden, while the shorter forms are great in pots and containers. My top choices include the silver-mauve 'Potomac Lavender' developed for cutting and a huge 1.2m (4ft) tall, while the rich crimson spikes of 'Liberty Classic Crimson' are perfect for the border at 60cm (24in) tall.

HOW TO GROW

A sunny spot and well-drained soil, enriched with some garden compost, is all that snapdragons need to thrive. They're strong growers, often becoming woody at the base and overwintering successfully for a few years. The taller varieties may need staking as they grow.

PROPAGATION

Sow seeds under cover in early spring, potting them on as they grow, and finally planting out after the frosts in May or June.

WILDLIFE VALUE

Snapdragons are good pollen plants for bees, especially. However, many F1 hybrids produce little or no pollen.

FASCINATING FACTS

Snapdragons have long been thought of as offering protection to the bearer, mainly due to their dragon-like appearance. The ancient Greeks and Romans believed the flowers protected them from witches, while they were often planted near the gates of European castles and manor houses as a ward of protection.

Cosmos

Pretty, showy and free-flowering

Latin name: *Cosmos* species and varieties

Plant type: Annual

Flower colour: Crimson, pink, white, yellow or orange

Flowering time: July to October

Easy to grow: Yes, more demanding to propagate

Height: 50cm–2m (20in to 6½ft)

Hardy: in USDA zones 2 to 11

Planting possibilities: Beds and borders, smaller varieties in containers

Growing conditions: Full sun, well-drained soil

Wildlife value: 4

GARDEN USE

Hailing from Mexico, cosmos are superb late-season border fillers. Use the flame colours of *Cosmos sulphureus*, which grows to 50cm (20in) tall, for a splash of heat in pots or borders. But, for the best show, plant the taller *Cosmos bipinnatus* varieties in the border or large pots, where their single or semi-double flowers in rich crimson, rosy pinks or clear white will complement other plants. My favourites include 'Seashells' with fluted petals, 'Versailles Tetra' with delicately shaded rich pink flowers, and 'Rubenza' with velvety red petals.

HOW TO GROW

These are true half-hardy annuals that won't tolerate any cold weather at the beginning or end of the season, so take care when planting them out. They all need a sunny spot and well-drained soil, and the taller varieties may need staking as they grow.

PROPAGATION

Sow seeds under cover in March or April, potting them on as they grow, and finally planting out after the frosts are over in May or June.

WILDLIFE VALUE

Cosmos are brilliant bee plants, especially, although they're also attractive to hoverflies, butterflies and some moths.

FASCINATING FACTS

Celebrated by Mexican priests as a symbol of harmony, cosmos was brought home to Madrid by Spanish explorers in the 16th century. The wife of the British ambassador in Spain then brought seeds to the UK in 1789, while it arrived in the USA around 50 years later.

Clematis

Easy climber with exquisite flowers

Flowering freely, beautifully and reliably, clematis is a plant that no garden should be without. Their uses are many and varied, and the flowers range from dainty soft pastels to plate-sized, rich velvet-purple or crimson showstoppers.

Latin name: *Clematis* species and varieties

Plant type: Climber

Flower colour: Purple, pink, blue or white

Flowering time: All year, depending on species – main season is summer

Easy to grow: Yes

Height: 2–10m (6½–33ft)

Hardy: in USDA zones 4 to 9

Planting possibilities: Arches, trellis, obelisks and grown through shrubs

Growing conditions: Full sun and some shade, well-drained soil

Wildlife value: 3

GARDEN USE

Not only are clematis beautiful, but they're also brilliant for hiding unsightly objects, whether that's a dilapidated shed, an ugly garage or an old tree stump. They're happy scrambling vigorously through obelisks, trellis or other garden plants as well, adding colour and beauty wherever they're planted. Use the vigorous spring-flowering varieties to cloak unsightly objects, while the more tender winter bloomers add interest out of season. But the main beauties are the summer types, with flowers large or small, bright or delicate.

FAVOURITE CLEMATIS

'Polish Spirit' is easy to grow and a brilliant sight in full flower, with a waterfall of rich purple-blue flowers from July to September.

'Nelly Moser' is the most tolerant, cheery clematis with its big candy-striped flowers in June and later again in September. It's a good choice for a north-facing wall, a low-light or shady situation as it will cope with happily and where the flowers will shine out.

'Blue Angel' produces masses of delicately ruffled, soft blue flowers and has a strong growing habit, which is great for arches and obelisks.

'Niobe' has large, velvet-red flowers and is lovely grown in a container in a shady spot, although it takes a little time and care to establish.

C. tangutica **'Bill MacKenzie'** has oriental-looking, nodding yellow flowers right the way through summer, followed by fantastically fluffy seed heads.

PLANTING PARTNERS

Plant summer-flowering clematis with roses for a winning combination, especially if growing on a trellis, arch or obelisk. Both plants seem to enjoy similar conditions, while the more vigorous clematis work well growing through trees. Use lower-growing shrubs and herbaceous plants to shade the roots of clematis, as they need to be cool and sheltered at the base to thrive.

HOW TO GROW

Clematis love to have cool, shaded roots, with the top growth preferring more sunshine. Mulch annually with well-rotted garden compost or manure.

PROPAGATION

Take stem cuttings about 10cm (4in) long from semi-ripe, non-flowering shoots in July.

WILDLIFE VALUE

Birds love the cover these thick, twiggy climbers provide, as well as the abundant seeds in autumn. Bees and hoverflies enjoy the pollen, too.

FASCINATING FACTS

'Old Man's Beard', a species of clematis named after its wispy seed heads, is native to Europe, and the thick, twining stems were used to bind crops and weave ropes and baskets.

Mock orange

Super-fragrant flowering shrub

Latin name: *Philadelphus* species and varieties

Plant type: Shrub

Flower colour: White

Flowering time: June

Easy to grow: Yes

Height: 1–2.5m (3–8ft)

Hardy: in USDA zones 4 to 7

Planting possibilities: Beds and borders

Growing conditions: Full sun or part shade, any soil

Wildlife value: 3

GARDEN USE

This easy-to-grow shrub scents the air in early summer with its gorgeously fragrant white flowers. Varieties like the robust 'Belle Étoile' with 5cm (2in) flowers, or the shorter double form 'Manteau d'Hermine', are the perfect addition to a mixed border, a cottage garden or a woodland border. The form 'Aureus' is a useful plant simply for its glowing foliage, although it also has small, scented flowers. It's happy planted in light shade, where the leaf colour is an attractive bright apple green.

HOW TO GROW

These are easy, strong-growing shrubs that are happy in a wide range of soils and in part shade or full sun.

PROPAGATION

Mock orange is easy to propagate from 7.5–10cm (3–4in) softwood cuttings taken in early summer from non-flowering shoots.

WILDLIFE VALUE

The single-flowered forms are very attractive to pollinators, especially bees.

FASCINATING FACTS

Lewis's mock orange, *Philadelphus lewisii*, is the state flower of Idaho, where it grows wild and is protected from collection by state law.

Iris

Exotic, ruffled flowers in gorgeous colourways

Irises range from the tiniest spring-flowering bulbs to tall, stately summer blooms, but one thing they all have in common is their beautiful flowers, which are like no others. In the case of the very early spring bulbs, the flowers pop up long before their leaves, their tiny blooms miniature versions of the summer showstoppers. These complicated flowers, large or small, are held above sword-like foliage and consist of three parts that come in different colourways and patterns and are often spotted and marked with 'beards'.

Latin name: *Iris* species and varieties

Plant type: Herbaceous perennial or bulb

Flower colour: Purple, pink, blue, yellow or white and variations

Flowering time: Summer, some bulbs in spring

Easy to grow: Yes

Height: 10–15cm (4–6in) for spring bulb varieties, 30cm–1.5m (12in–5ft) for perennials

Hardy: in USDA zones 3 to 9

Planting possibilities: Beds and borders

Growing conditions: Full sun, soil dependent on species

Wildlife value: 3

GARDEN USE

Irises deserve a spot in every garden, especially the summer-flowering varieties, bearded or not. These all make good border plants, with their striking leaves adding contrast and structure, even before the flowers appear. With a wealth of colours, patterns and heights to pick from, choosing an iris for a scheme is a joy. Use the sun-loving bearded types in a drier, sunnier border, and the Siberian irises in damper, shadier situations and near ponds.

FAVOURITE IRISES

'Jane Phillips' is a classic bearded iris choice, with its enchanting sky-blue flowers held at about 1m (3ft) tall above grey foliage. Flowering in late May and June, it looks ethereal planted en masse or lining a border.

'Braithwaite' is a bearded iris with flowers that make for an eye-catching show in the border. They combine rich velvet-purple falls with soft lilac standards around 80cm (31in) tall above grey-green leaves.

'Raspberry Blush' is a dwarf bearded iris growing only 50cm (20in) tall with pretty, dusky-pink flowers.

'Tropic Night' is a Siberian iris that produces masses of delicately veined, rich purple flowers held above strappy green foliage about 1m (3ft) tall.

'Sparkling Rose' is a Siberian variety with lilac-pink petals, veined with white and touched with yellow at the base.

PLANTING PARTNERS

Bearded iris varieties grow well with other perennials such as salvia, lupins, peonies and oriental poppies. They also look great with shrubs, including roses and *Euphorbia*, and with taller plants like foxgloves and alliums. For a gravel garden, plant them with dry-loving grasses such as stipa, and sun-loving shrubs like lavender and other Mediterranean herbs.

HOW TO GROW

Bearded irises love a sunny spot, where the rhizomes at the base of the plant are kept warm and well-drained. Siberian irises will tolerate a wider range of soils, including damp soils at the edge of a pond, and are happy in sun or part shade.

PROPAGATION

Divide the rhizomes of bearded and Siberian irises carefully in July or August after they have finished flowering.

WILDLIFE VALUE

Irises are attractive to bees especially, as their falls provide good pathways to their pollen.

FASCINATING FACTS

Iris means 'rainbow' in ancient Greek, which is appropriate as the flowers come in such a wealth and variety of colours. An extract of iris, orris root, is used in perfumes and for flavouring gin.

Sweet pea

Fragrant and fabulous for cutting

Latin name: *Lathyrus odoratus*

Plant type: Annual

Flower colour: All colours except yellow, often bicoloured

Flowering time: June to September

Easy to grow: Yes

Height: 50cm–2.5m (20in–8ft)

Hardy: in USDA zones 3 to 8

Planting possibilities: Beds and borders, cutting garden, arches and obelisks

Growing conditions: Full sun, any soil except dry

Wildlife value: 4

GARDEN USE

These classic annual climbers are great garden plants, but they're just as at home on the allotment, pulling in pollinators and providing plenty of flowers for cutting. Grow them simply up netting or trellis, or over an arch, while the shorter varieties also look good in a pot. My favourite sweet peas for scent are 'High Scent' with very fragrant, delicate cream flowers edged with lilac; 'Erewhon' with pink and blue flowers; and 'Matucana', an ancient variety with violet and crimson bicoloured flowers. For cutting, go for pure white 'Valentine', the strong pink 'Dynasty' or 'Blue Velvet', which is a rich velvet-blue with long stems. 'Lavender Sprite' is a dwarf variety that grows only 50cm (20cm) or so tall and is great for small gardens and containers.

HOW TO GROW

Sweet peas need a cool, moist root area that is kept regularly watered in dry weather, but they also like a sunny spot to produce the best flowering. Avoid wet or waterlogged soils, and soil that is dry should be enriched with a good mulch of garden compost or well-rotted manure before planting. Pick or deadhead regularly to keep the flowers coming.

PROPAGATION

Sow seeds indoors or in a cold frame from September to April. Plant the seeds singly in deep pots where the roots can develop strongly.

WILDLIFE VALUE

The mass of flowers over a long period attracts pollinators such as hoverflies and bees.

FASCINATING FACTS

A Sicilian monk, Franciscus Cupani, introduced the annual sweet pea to the UK in the late 17th century, and the variety 'Cupani' is the closest to the original species.

In the USA, sweet peas became hugely popular, both as garden plants and as cut flowers. By the late 1800s, Californian growers were shipping sweet peas all over the country by train.

Salvia

Pretty lipped flowers that are a boon for pollinators

With new varieties coming from plant breeders and their value for wildlife, salvias have become an essential part of garden planting. While they look like their sister plant, sage, and share its fragrant foliage, these easy-to-grow plants come in a variety of shapes and sizes and a good array of colours. Even when not in full flower, their leafy, fragrant foliage adds substance to the border, and many also grow well in pots.

Latin name: *Salvia* species and varieties

Plant type: Herbaceous perennial, shrub or annual

Flower colour: Purple, pink, blue or white, often bicoloured

Flowering time: Summer and early autumn

Easy to grow: Yes

Height: 20cm (8in) for annual varieties, up to 2m (6½ft) for perennials

Hardy: in USDA zones 3 to 9

Planting possibilities: Beds and borders, gravel garden, pots and containers

Growing conditions: Full sun, well-drained soil

Wildlife value: 4

GARDEN USE

Salvias have a wealth of uses in the garden, ranging from small annual varieties for bedding schemes to the tall, late-flowering herbaceous varieties that can make a real statement in the late summer and early autumn border. Use the sun-loving perennial forms of *Salvia nemorosa* in dry gardens with grasses, while many of the annuals make good bedding plants or cut flowers. But it's the rounded, shrubby varieties with their small but brilliantly coloured flowers that are the best value in the garden, flowering all summer long. 'Hot Lips' is the one you'll commonly find, but look for other, more colourful varieties.

FAVOURITE SALVIAS

'Cerro Potosi' is a rich, deep pink, shrubby variety that is slightly taller than some, with long flower spikes and a nicely branching habit.

'Nachtvlinder' has deep purple flowers set off against the green foliage. It's a great choice for pots, where its shrubby shape balances taller plants.

'Blue Note' is another good shrubby choice for pots, with clear blue flowers.

'Caradonna' is a *Salvia nemorosa* type that thrives in drier soils and produces spikes of brilliant red and purple flowers en masse in early summer.

Salvia horminum, or clary sage, is an annual with brilliantly coloured and veined bracts. It makes a great addition to the border and is good for cutting and drying.

'Amistad' is a statuesque herbaceous variety that flowers late in the season, with tall spikes of midnight-purple flowers.

PLANTING PARTNERS

There is a salvia for almost anywhere in the garden, except shade. The little shrubs make the perfect counterpoint to the big, blousy flowers of roses, as well as working well with annuals and summer bedding plants to keep pots looking lovely for months on end. Plant the sun lovers with stipa grasses, *Eryngium* and *Perovskia*, while the tall 'Amistad' looks great with other tender plants like dahlias and cannas for a tropical look.

HOW TO GROW

All salvias love a sunny spot with warm and well-drained soil. They need shelter from cold winds, and some are tender and will need winter protection or to be overwintered as rooted cuttings.

PROPAGATION

In summer, take cuttings from non-flowering shoots and root them in a gritty, well-drained compost. Sow the seeds of annual varieties in spring in pots for later planting, or directly where they are to grow.

WILDLIFE VALUE

All salvias are beneficial to pollinators, especially bees.

FASCINATING FACTS

Sage, *Salvia officinalis*, has long been used as a culinary herb, but it also has a long history for use in herbal remedies by the ancient Greeks, Romans, Native Americans and in Chinese medicine.

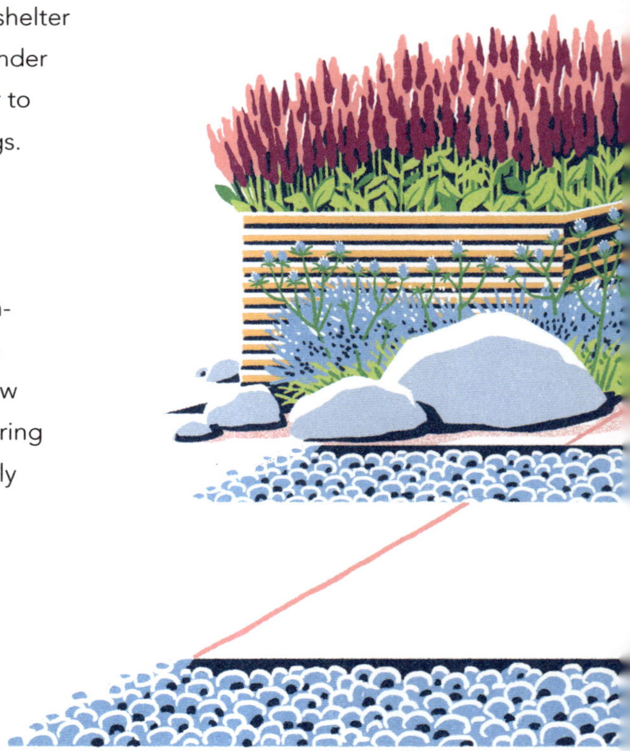

Foxglove

Towering spires of spotted flowers

Latin name: *Digitalis* species and varieties

Plant type: Biennial or herbaceous perennial

Flower colour: Common variety is white or purple, some perennials are yellow, pink or orange

Flowering time: June

Easy to grow: Yes

Height: 60cm–2m (2–6½ft)

Hardy: in USDA zones 4 to 7

Planting possibilities: Beds and borders

Growing conditions: Full sun and part shade, moist soil

Wildlife value: 4

GARDEN USE

The majestic purple or white spires of the common foxglove stand out in the border in early summer, adding stature to the garden and helpfully self-seeding to create some winning surprise combinations. Perennial varieties, such as *Digitalis lutea* with yellow flowers and *Digitalis parviflora*, a sun-lover with densely packed stems of dark orange flowers, tend to be shorter than the common foxglove, but make interesting additions to a mixed border.

HOW TO GROW

Foxgloves are happy in moist soil and in partial shade or full sun. The common foxglove is tolerant of poor soils and sunny locations, but dappled shade is the ideal.

PROPAGATION

Foxgloves self-seed when happy, and the seedlings can be easily transplanted when young. Alternatively, collect and sow the seeds into pots.

WILDLIFE VALUE

Foxgloves are brilliant pollen sources for bees, especially bumblebees, while several moth caterpillars feed on the flowers and foliage.

FASCINATING FACTS

According to folklore, the foxglove is so named because foxes wore the flowers on their paws to silence them while hunting. This probably came about because foxglove flowers often grow in the disturbed soil close to fox dens.

What to do in the garden during summer

There are some key tasks that need attending to early in the season, before the garden runs amok. It's vital to get a grip on staking, deadheading and pest management. That means getting your structures in place long before the stems are gaining height, whether you're using woven pea sticks or shop-bought frames. Doing this early allows the plants to grow through the frames naturally, avoiding the need to truss them up when they're already well grown, which looks somewhat messy. As the long, hot days of summer wear on, keep your eyes open for your plants suffering any signs of stress, as this is often when pests will get a grip on a failing plant. Look out for wilting foliage, browning leaves and flowers fading almost as soon as they open. Usually a good water and perhaps a feed at the right time can avert more serious problems, but it's a matter of spotting the symptoms. Sitting back and relaxing is obviously an essential task at this time of the year too, and it does give you a chance to look long and hard at the garden, watching out for anything untoward occurring.

It's tempting to water frequently, but most plants respond better to a thorough watering less often. Soak wilting shrubs and trees once or twice a week, letting the water seep into the ground at the roots for 15 minutes or so.

Plants in pots and containers are completely reliant on you for water and will need more frequent attention. Make sure you water thoroughly, though, as compost can often shrink, allowing the water to simply run down the inside of the pot without actually wetting the compost significantly. Place smaller pots in a tray or saucer to give them a good soak, but don't leave them sitting in water.

Plant out tender plants such as bedding favourites *Pelargonium* and cosmos, as well as dahlias and cannas, early in summer, getting any supports and frames in place almost immediately.

Encourage natural slug and snail control by bringing birds into pest-prone areas of the garden, for example where you have lots of dahlias. Place bird tables or feeders nearby, or interplant with seed-bearing grasses and annuals like amaranth and sunflowers.

Summer is a good time to plant out any seedling annuals and biennials like honesty and foxgloves. They'll settle in nicely, put on some growth and overwinter to give strong, early-flowering plants. Of course, left to its own devices, nature will already be doing some of this job for you, naturally seeding plants around the garden.

Deadhead regularly to keep new flowers coming. All plants benefit from deadheading, but especially the prolific bloomers like roses, cosmos, dahlias and sweet peas. Snip off the old flowers, ideally cutting the stem down to the next branching point, which is where new flower stems will appear. As we get towards the end of the season, leave some flowers to set seed so you can collect them and as a place for the birds to gather.

Autumn

The early days of autumn or fall are often soft, warm, but somewhat dampened by rains. This makes for a super show of flowers, set off by emerald-green grass and slanting sunshine. My sunniest border has a prairie-style planting of grasses that positively glow in the autumn light, studded with *Echinacea* and *Rudbeckia*, and offering plenty of late-season nectar for pollinators. The repeat-flowering roses will put on a final show, complementing late herbaceous performers like penstemons and rusty red sedum. But the stars of the early autumn garden are the glamorous dahlias and svelte cosmos. With regular deadheading they'll keep on flowering until winter arrives and the first frosts stop them in their tracks.

As we get into late autumn, those last balmy days fade away and everything seems to slow and close down; the leaves begin to turn, the frosts hover at night and the plants draw into themselves. There are still plants that flower only now, though, and mid-autumn is when the Michaelmas daisies have their moment. Their pastel colours may not demand attention like dahlias, but they look wonderful with grasses.

Leaves are a constant through autumn, with the cherry leaves turning spectacular colours then falling to the ground in flurries as a storm hits or, in the case of the wisteria, in sudden frost-induced dumps. Set off against the colourful leaves, the late flowers of shrubs like hydrangeas and fuchsias come into their own and the hydrangea flower heads will often dry to create a sepia-toned display that will last into winter.

Dahlia

Classy, colourful and exuberant bloomers

These gloriously flamboyant flowers are a radiant addition to any garden, flowering for long periods and plentifully from late summer through to the first frosts of autumn. Fortunately, they're easy to grow and look after, which means they'll be back to flower just as brilliantly next season.

Latin name: *Dahlia* species and varieties

Plant type: Half-hardy tuberous perennial

Flower colour: All colours, including multi-coloured varieties

Flowering time: Late July or early August until frost

Easy to grow: Yes

Height: 30cm–1.5m (12in–5ft), depending on variety

Hardy: in USDA zones 8 to 10

Planting possibilities: Beds and borders, cutting garden, pots and containers

Growing conditions: Full sun, well-drained soil, shelter from cold winds

Wildlife value: 3

GARDEN USE

Varying from the small bedding varieties to the enormous giant forms with flowers some 20cm (8in) or more across, there is a dahlia to suit every garden and every gardener's taste. As well as superb garden plants, they make brilliant cut flowers, producing all the more flowers when you cut them regularly. The worst thing about dahlias is that they are hugely attractive to slugs and snails, but this is mainly a problem in spring and early summer when the plants are smaller, so provided you can keep these pests under control, your dahlias should thrive. The largest flowered varieties are best used for showing, but among the thousands of varieties available, there is a myriad of shapes, forms, colours and sizes to choose from. So many that it's hard to pick favourites.

FAVOURITE DAHLIAS

'Waltzing Mathilda' is one I return to year after year for its glowing, soft pink-orange flowers set off by rich dark foliage. It's a nicely mid-sized plant with a good, strong growth habit, and its semi-double flowers are perfect for pollinators, too.

'Café au Lait' always appeals to the pastel lovers and florists with its large, soft flowers of ivory, latte and a hint of pink.

'Blue Bayou' has flattened, anemone-like, mauve-blue flowers that the plant produces in profusion and are attractive to pollinators, especially butterflies.

'Orfeo' is a personal favourite as it's the first dahlia I ever grew, and it's a beauty with vibrant, rich purple cactus-type flowers on strong stems.

'Doris Day' is another favourite as I'm a fan of both the actress and the flower. It's sturdy, neat and produces masses of small, cactus-type flowers in a vivid shade of red – just the colour of Doris Day's lipstick.

'Happy Single' series are easy to grow with single flowers in an array of colours. The single blooms offer pollen and nectar to insects, and they're sturdy enough to need minimal staking.

PLANTING PARTNERS

In the garden, dahlias mix well with established perennials and shrubs to add a vibrant show in late summer, often benefiting from other plants for some support. However, these other plants can often harbour slugs and snails, so if these are a particular problem, plant your dahlias intermingled with grasses to encourage birds that will feed on the seeds and the slugs. Alternatively, because of the great array of colours, they look good planted simply with other dahlia varieties or annuals to create a cutting garden or border.

HOW TO GROW

Plant rooted cuttings or sprouted tubers in May after the risk of frost has passed, staking them as they grow and protecting them from slugs and snails, especially in the early season. After frost has blackened the foliage in October or November, cut the stems back to 5–10cm (2–4in), either leaving them in the ground with a mulch of compost or lifting them, drying them, and potting them in dry compost to store indoors over winter.

PROPAGATION

Take 7cm (2¾in) cuttings from basal shoots in spring or from non-flowering shoots later in the summer. They root readily and will make flowering-size plants in a season. Alternatively, divide the tubers in March.

WILDLIFE VALUE

Single and semi-double forms of dahlia provide an important late-season source of food for bees, flies, butterflies and beetles.

FASCINATING FACTS

There are now more than 57,000 registered varieties of dahlia, with new forms added to the official list each year.

Coneflower

Brilliantly coloured daisies

Latin name: *Echinacea purpurea*

Plant type: Perennial

Flower colour: Purple, magenta, orange or white

Flowering time: July to September

Easy to grow: Yes

Height: 50cm–1.5m (20in–5ft)

Hardy: in USDA zones 3 to 9

Planting possibilities: Beds and borders

Growing conditions: Full sun, well-drained soil

Wildlife value: 4

GARDEN USE

Native to the USA, where it grows wild in prairies, this is a stalwart for the late-summer border. The species itself has tall stems topped with rich magenta-purple petals or ray florets, with cone-shaped, orange centres that are tough and spiny, hence the name *Echinacea,* after the Latin name for sea urchin. These spiny cones persist long into the autumn after the petals have faded and dropped off, leaving a bristling seed head to add interest to the late-autumn border.

Echinaceas combine well with grasses for a prairie-style planting or with other later flowering perennials, such as *Rudbeckia*. Although they're available in a range of colours, from the red-petalled 'Tomato Ketchup' to the dainty, thin orange petals of 'Art's Pride', their beauty isn't always equal to their resilience. For sheer robustness, my favourites are 'White Swan', pure white with golden centres, and 'Magnus', strong, vibrantly coloured, and very like the native species.

HOW TO GROW

Choose a well-drained spot, south or southwest facing, as *Echinaceas* like to be a little on the dry side. Likewise, the front of a border is best, in full sun or very light shade.

PROPAGATION

Sow seeds in spring or, alternatively, divide and replant the roots when the plant is dormant between October and March.

WILDLIFE VALUE

Bees and butterflies love the readily available nectar and pollen, while birds enjoy the seeds later in autumn.

FASCINATING FACTS

Native American used *Echinacea* for over 400 years to treat a variety of ailments, including infections, wounds and snake bites.

Michaelmas daisy

Autumnal daisies in an array of soft colours

Michaelmas daisies are simply a must-have plant for the autumn garden. Short, tall, single or double, in shades of blue, purple, pink or white, these versatile plants flower so well and for so long that they make a brilliant show just by themselves. They seem a bit confusing at first glance, as what was once a single group known as *Asters* is now divided into several different groups. As well as *Aster*, now a distinct species, the group contains two main types, *Symphyotrichum* and *Eurybia*, which are known as wood asters as they prefer shade. All are great garden plants, although the classic Michaelmas daisies are more versatile and varied in their forms and varieties. Steer clear of the *Symphyotrichum novi-belgii* forms, if possible, as they're prone to disfiguring mildew, while the New England varieties, *Symphyotrichum novae-angliae*, are healthier.

Latin name: *Aster*, *Symphyotrichum* and *Eurybia* species and varieties

Plant type: Herbaceous perennial

Flower colour: Blue, pink, purple or white

Flowering time: Late July to November, depending on species

Easy to grow: Yes

Height: 30cm–1.5m (12in–5ft), depending on variety

Hardy: in USDA zones 4 to 9

Planting possibilities: Beds and borders, cutting garden, pots and containers

Growing conditions: Full sun, well-drained soil, shelter from winds

Wildlife value: 4

FAVOURITE MICHAELMAS DAISIES

Aster **'King George'** is a personal favourite for its violet-blue, yellow-centred single flowers some 5cm (2in) across that are an irresistible magnet for butterflies in August and September. Compared to many others, it's a nicely mid-sized plant that reaches only 45–55cm (17¾–21½in) tall, which makes it ideal for the border.

Symphyotrichum **'Calliope'** is another favourite, especially for a more natural-style planting, where its tiny mauve flowers dotted on arching dark stems up to 1.5m (5ft) or so tall look loose and lovely planted with grasses.

Symphyotrichum **'Tonga'** is a little sweetie for pots, containers and the very front of a border. Growing only 40cm (16in) tall, nonetheless its rich purple flowers are a splash of vivid colour. The 'Island' series are all short and easy to grow, but 'Tonga' has the best colour.

Symphyotrichum **'Little Carlow'** is perhaps the most commonly seen variety, and rightly so, as it's easy to grow, a nice size at around 90cm (35in) tall, and produces masses of beautiful blue flowers in autumn.

Eurybia x herveyi **or** ***Aster*** **'Twilight'** has soft purple single flowers in August and September. It's especially useful as it prefers light or dappled shade, and it looks great in a woodland border setting.

GARDEN USE

There's a Michaelmas daisy to suit every garden, whether that's short and colourful for pots and containers or tall, stately and more muted in colour for the back of a border. Most varieties make great cut flowers, and they work well with other plants, demanding little effort and attention from the gardener.

PLANTING PARTNERS

You can use Michaelmas daisies in a traditional cottage garden way, planting them with annuals such as sweet peas and cornflowers, or bring them bang up to date by combining the tall forms with dainty daisy flowers with tall grasses. Alternatively, pot the smaller forms up on their own, or mix them in bedding schemes, while the shade lovers are a useful addition to woodland borders. The use of these plants is only limited by your imagination. My favourite way to grow them is in a border with a hydrangea or two, grasses and other autumn perennials. That will give you a garden that will look good until the frosts start.

HOW TO GROW

Most Michaelmas daisies need a sunny spot, unless they're the woodland *Eurybia* types, and they're forgiving if the soil isn't the best quality. Make sure they don't dry out in late summer, just as they're coming into flower, especially as the *Symphyotrichum novi-belgii* varieties are prone to mildew. Add an organic mulch of garden compost in between the plants towards the end of the year and split the clumps every few years to rejuvenate them.

PROPAGATION

Dividing established clumps in spring is by far the easiest method of propagation. However, you can also take cuttings early in spring.

WILDLIFE VALUE

Single forms of Michaelmas daisies are wonderful for all sorts of pollinators, from hoverflies and bees to butterflies and moths.

FASCINATING FACTS

Michaelmas daisies are so-called as they're often in flower on St. Michael's Day at the end of September. In Christian tradition, the Archangel is regarded as the protector from darkness and evil, and the flowers help to push back the gloom of winter.

Penstemon *or* beardtongue

Spikes of colourful, snapdragon-like flowers

Latin name: *Penstemon* species and varieties

Plant type: Herbaceous perennial

Flower colour: Purple, mauve, red, pink and white, often bicoloured

Flowering time: July to November

Easy to grow: Easy

Height: 50cm–1.5m (20in–5ft)

Hardy: in USDA zones 3 to 9

Planting possibilities: Beds and borders

Growing conditions: Full sun, any soil

Wildlife value: 4

GARDEN USE

Penstemons are brilliantly reliable, flowering for weeks if regularly deadheaded, and pack a lot of flower and colour into one plant. They have a brilliant ability to go well with all sorts of other plants, looking just as good in a modern, prairie-style border with grasses and other perennials as they do with cottage garden favourites. They'll cope with drier conditions, too, and are often used for gravel and dry gardens. Look for *Penstemon* 'Andenken an Friedrich Hahn', more commonly known as 'Garnet', and the 'Bird' series with their rich dark flowers.

HOW TO GROW

Penstemons need sunshine and shelter to perform at their best. Avoid waterlogged soil and shady, chilly locations.

PROPAGATION

Penstemons root very readily from cuttings taken from non-flowering shoots in summer.

WILDLIFE VALUE

The characteristically tubular flowers of beardtongues are good for many pollinators such as bumblebees, as well as moths, butterflies and wasps. In the USA, hummingbirds are also attracted to them, particularly to the red-flowered species.

FASCINATING FACTS

Penstemon species are prolific in the USA, and the epicentre is the state of Utah, which is home to a whopping 70 species. In fact, except for one species, penstemons do not occur naturally outside North America.

Hydrangea

Flamboyant, flouncy heads of flowers

Pick the right variety for your taste and a hydrangea will give you pleasure for years to come. That's quite a task as there are so many lovely hydrangea species and varieties, that picking only one or two is difficult. These shrubs, as well as some climbing forms, are the perfect combination of showy, bright and easy-to-grow, making them ideal garden plants. If you're lucky enough to garden on acidic soil, many will produce wonderfully dramatic azure flowers, while most are shades of pink, white or mauve. They start flowering in summer, but many age and fade beautifully, with the robust flower heads withstanding weather and cold to give a good show into autumn.

Latin name: *Hydrangea* species and varieties

Plant type: Shrub or climber

Flower colour: Blue, pink, mauve or white

Flowering time: July to October, depending on species

Easy to grow: Yes

Height: 50cm–2.5m (20in–8ft), depending on species or variety

Hardy: in USDA zones 3 to 9, depending on species

Planting possibilities: Beds and borders, cutting garden, pots and containers

Growing conditions: Full sun, part shade, well-drained soil, shelter from cold winds

Wildlife value: 2

GARDEN USE

Hydrangeas can be very versatile and work well in many gardens. Small varieties add interest in smaller gardens and courtyards and look great in pots, while the larger growing forms are good for big gardens and woodland-style plantings. Use climbing forms to clothe shady walls, where the creamy white flowers will brighten up a dark corner. On acidic soils, some shrub varieties have striking blue flowers, while on neutral soils the colour will be mauve and, on alkaline soils, pink.

FAVOURITE HYDRANGEAS

Hydrangea quercifolia is a brilliant, late-flowering plant for a woodland-style border, with large, oakleaf foliage that often turns lovely colours in autumn or fall, with panicles of creamy flowers.

Madame Emile Mouillère' is a mid-sized classic hydrangea with large mopheads of white flowers.

'Limelight' is a favourite, with sturdy growth up to 2.5m (8ft) tall, and panicles of lime green and white flowers that age to pink shades as they fade later in the autumn. It's especially useful for a more relaxed, natural-style planting where it blends well with other late-season shrubs and perennials.

'Little Lime' is a smaller version of 'Limelight' with all the character but in a diminutive form, which makes it great for pots and small gardens.

'Lanarth' series have flattened, lacecap-style flowers on well-behaved, medium-sized shrubs.

PLANTING PARTNERS

Hydrangeas go well with other shade lovers such as leafy ferns and hostas, as well as hellebores. They also look great planted with other hydrangea varieties and forms, and if you have an acidic soil, plant them with rhododendrons and azaleas. I like them with hardy geraniums for a softer, more cottage garden look.

HOW TO GROW

Given a sheltered spot and good soil, most hydrangeas should thrive. They need protection from frost and leaving the flower heads on the plant through winter helps with this, as well as adding interest to the garden. They're tolerant of most soils, except dry and thin, and prefer one that's rich in organic matter, so give your plants a regular mulch.

PROPAGATION

Take cuttings from non-flowering shoots in late summer. They should be firm and slightly woody at the base, but with a soft tip for best results.

WILDLIFE VALUE

The dense growth of these shrubs provides good shelter for small mammals and birds, while the flowers of some species and varieties are good for pollinators.

FASCINATING FACTS

Most *Hydrangea* species, and there are more than 70 of them, are native to Japan, China and Korea. They have been cultivated in Japan for centuries and feature prolifically in ancient paintings and poetry.

Nerine *or* Guernsey lily

Exotic late-season flowers

Latin name: *Nerine bowdenii*

Plant type: Bulb

Flower colour: Red, pink or white

Flowering time: August to November

Easy to grow: More demanding of care

Height: 30–60cm (12–24in)

Hardy: in USDA zones 8 to 11

Planting possibilities: Beds and borders, cutting garden, pots and containers

Growing conditions: Full sun, well-drained soil, shelter from cold winds essential

Wildlife value: 1

GARDEN USE

These spectacular bulbs add such a splash of colour to the autumn garden that they are well worth any fuss they may demand. Native to South Africa and widely grown as a cut flower in the Channel Islands, most species and varieties are best planted in pots where they can grow in the shelter and warmth of a greenhouse. But *Nerine bowdenii* is hardy when planted at the base of a sun-trapped wall, where the bulbs can bake in summer and aren't overshadowed by other plants, and where the exotic flowers make a brilliant show in autumn. 'Vesta K' has soft pink flowers some 20cm (8in) across, while 'Mr John' has vibrant, rosy-red flowers.

HOW TO GROW

Nerine bowdenii needs a sunny, well-drained spot in the garden and a good mulch after flowering to protect the bulbs from cold. All varieties do very well in pots, appreciating good drainage and light watering through the winter, when the bulbs are dormant.

PROPAGATION

Plant dry bulbs in summer, potting them first to develop a root system before planting out, or plant directly into a suitable spot. Established clumps can be lifted and divided after four or five years.

WILDLIFE VALUE

No notable wildlife value.

FASCINATING FACTS

According to an ancient story, a ship carrying these bulbs to the Netherlands was shipwrecked on the shores of Guernsey in the English Channel. The boxes of bulbs washed up on the shoreline and the bulbs subsequently rooted and established, multiplying and becoming known as the Guernsey lily.

Black-eyed Susan

Bright yellow, chocolate-centred daisies

Latin name: *Rudbeckia* species and varieties

Plant type: Annual or herbaceous perennial

Flower colour: Usually yellow, sometimes orange or copper-brown

Flowering time: July to October

Easy to grow: Yes

Height: 25cm–2.5m (10in–8ft)

Hardy: in USDA zones 3 to 9

Planting possibilities: Beds and borders, cutting garden, smaller varieties in containers

Growing conditions: Full sun, well-drained soil

Wildlife value: 4

GARDEN USE

Bold, showy and available in all sizes, *Rudbeckia* species and varieties are a must-have for borders, pots, bedding and prairie-style planting. There are few plants more reliable and versatile in the late -summer garden, although the rich golden yellows of the perennial varieties aren't always the easiest to match with other plants. You can't go wrong if you use a yolk-yellow, medium-sized variety such as 'Goldsturm' with grasses and other prairie species like *Echinacea*. Taller varieties such as 'Herbstonne' can reach 1.5–2.5m (5–8ft) tall with swept-back, golden yellow petals, while 'Goldquelle' is a more restrained 1m (3ft) tall. At the other end of the spectrum, at 25cm (10in) tall, the tiny 'Toto' makes a great plant for pots and containers. Annuals include the rich wine-red 'Cherry Brandy', which I find a bit slow to get flowering, and 'Prairie Sun' with orange-flushed petals.

Even after the petals have faded, the chocolate brown, or sometimes green, centres persist into the late autumn and winter, adding interest to the garden.

HOW TO GROW

Choose a well-drained spot, a good, rich soil, and an open, sunny situation, although be aware that if it's too open you may have to stake plants to support them. That's definitely true of the taller perennial species and often true of the annuals, too. Handily for gardeners, *Rudbeckias* are rabbit and deer resistant.

PROPAGATION

Sow seeds of both annual and perennial species in spring or, preferably, divide and replant roots of perennials when the plant is dormant between October and March.

WILDLIFE VALUE

Bees and butterflies love the readily available nectar and pollen, while birds feed on the seeds later in autumn.

FASCINATING FACTS

Many species of *Rudbeckia* are used in prairie restoration in the USA, where conservation is concentrated on restoring prairie lands that were destroyed due to farming and industrial use.

Chrysanthemum

Take your pick of pompom or daisy, bright or pastel

Chrysanthemums have had something of a renaissance recently. Once dismissed as somewhat old-fashioned – although retaining popularity in China and with florists worldwide – they're now being appreciated anew for their versatility, lovely colours and long flowering period. Some varieties are best grown indoors for at least part of the year, which many gardeners have regarded as far too troublesome to bother with. One look at the flouncy show varieties and you can see why, but some make good garden plants, with minimum fuss required.

Latin name: *Chrysanthemum* species and varieties

Plant type: Annual or perennial

Flower colour: From white and yellow through orange and red to pink and purple

Flowering time: September until frost

Easy to grow: Yes

Height: 50cm–1m (20in–3ft)

Hardy: in USDA zones 4 to 9

Planting possibilities: Beds and borders, cutting garden, pots and containers

Growing conditions: Full sun, well-drained soil, shelter from cold winds

Wildlife value: 2

GARDEN USE

Chrysanthemums are surprisingly versatile in a garden setting. Use them in a formal way, such as in a bedding scheme, or informally in the border with other late-flowering plants. They work superbly in containers, as many varieties have a nice, bushy, compact habit, and they go well with autumnal plants such as *Gaultheria*, *Cyclamen*, pansies and violas. An obvious use is in a cut flower border or garden, as chrysanthemums are a mainstay of floristry, lasting for long periods once cut. The brighter, bolder varieties will even blend well with leafy, exotic plantings, adding a splash of late colour to a scheme.

FAVOURITE GARDEN CHRYSANTHEMUMS

'Dixter Orange' has super, rusty orange, double flowers on sturdy stems up to 80cm (31in) tall. It goes nicely with lots of other plants and is mid-sized with a good, strong growth that seems to cope with most winters.

'Jolie Rose' has pretty single pink flowers with golden yellow centres, set off by a lovely white ring at the base of the petals. It's sturdy, a useful 60cm (24in) tall, and it keeps on flowering right until the frosts finish it off.

Brennpunkt' is vivid blood-red with hints of copper. Growing up to 80cm (31in) tall, it makes a great foil to lush leaves and wispy grasses.

PLANTING PARTNERS

In the garden, chrysanthemums look great with other late-flowering plants such as salvias and Michaelmas daisies, and especially grasses. Plant the pastel varieties with cottage garden favourites such as hardy annuals like nigella, cornflowers and sweet peas, while the dramatic red forms look wonderful set against lush foliage such as canna, fatsia and hosta. All look great with floaty grasses like *Stipa tenuissima* and *Panicum*, and the red and orange ones go especially well with the autumnal tones of pheasant grass *Anemanthele lessoniana*.

HOW TO GROW

Chrysanthemums love a warm, sheltered, sunny location with fertile, well-drained soil. Avoid shade, waterlogged soil and any cold spots, as the plants won't cope with these conditions at all. Mulch them in autumn to give added protection over winter.

PROPAGATION

Take basal cuttings from new shoots in spring or early summer. If you're at all worried about overwintering plants outside, it's a good idea to take a handful of cuttings, just in case.

WILDLIFE VALUE

Single and semi-double varieties are good for bees and other pollinators.

FASCINATING FACTS

Chrysanthemums have been cultivated and appreciated in China for centuries, where they feature in artworks and poetry dating back some 3,000 years. Japan has a National Chrysanthemum Day in September, which is also known as the Festival of Happiness.

Hardy fuchsia

Dancing flowers on easy-to-grow shrubs

Latin name: *Fuchsia* species and varieties

Plant type: Shrub

Flower colour: Red, orange, purple, pink and white flowers, often bicoloured

Flowering time: July to October

Easy to grow: Yes

Height: 50cm–1.5m (20in–5ft), depending on variety

Hardy: in USDA zones 5 to 7, but will die in colder zones during the winter

Planting possibilities: Beds and borders, pots and containers

Growing conditions: Full sun, light shade, well-drained soil, shelter from cold winds

Wildlife value: 3

GARDEN USE

Reaching their height of popularity during the 19th century, many fuchsias, both hardy and tender varieties, are still widely used for bedding displays and hanging baskets. But, although somewhat out of fashion, the hardy forms are incredibly useful long-flowering structural shrubs for the late-summer and autumn garden. Keep the blousy ballerina varieties such as 'Dollar Princess' for pots and baskets, and opt for the hardier, smaller flowered types such as 'Lady Boothby' and the simple white 'Hawkshead' for the garden. Combine them with perennials and grasses in the border or use them as an informal flowering hedge in a sheltered city garden or warmer area.

HOW TO GROW

Larger varieties make perfect well-behaved border shrubs, provided they have a sheltered spot away from cold winds and shade. They can cope with a little shade, but a sunny spot is better with good soil that doesn't get waterlogged. In a hard winter, the growth may die back to the ground, but established plants will re-emerge strongly from the base in the spring, especially if treated to a protective mulch through the winter.

PROPAGATION

Take tip cuttings from non-flowering shoots in March and they should root easily with a little bottom heat.

WILDLIFE VALUE

Single-flowered forms are good for pollinators with long tongues, such as butterflies, moths and some species of bee. Hummingbirds are also fond of the tubular flowers. Fuchsias are a good food source for caterpillars – in fact, I've seen more elephant hawkmoth caterpillars on fuchsias than anything else.

FASCINATING FACTS

You can eat the berries of fuchsias, although some are rather dull. The best tasting is *Fuchsia splendens*, which tastes of citrus and black pepper, and some varieties are selected especially for their fruit.

Sedum *or* ice plant

Easy, colourful and long-lasting

Latin name: *Hylotelephium* or *Sedum* species and varieties

Plant type: Perennial

Flower colour: Shades of pink and white

Flowering time: July to October

Easy to grow: Yes

Height: 10–50cm (4–20in)

Hardy: in USDA zones 3 to 11

Planting possibilities: Beds and borders

Growing conditions: Full sun, light shade, well-drained to dry soil

Wildlife value: 5

GARDEN USE

With their colour-drenched, flattened flower heads packed with starry little flowers, these plants make a long-lasting impact in the late summer and autumnal garden. They combine well with all sorts of late-flowering perennials, such as Michaelmas daisies, penstemon, *Rudbeckia* and many others. Earlier in the season the succulent leaves, which can be blue-grey, purple or variegated, look wonderfully structural as they grow and develop. After flowering the rusty flower heads persist into winter, adding interest to the garden. My favourites include 'Brilliant' with bright pink flowers, and 'Stardust' with fresh white flowers set off by grey-green foliage.

HOW TO GROW

These plants are perfect for a poorer, drier, more alkaline soil in full sun, although they can tolerate some very light shade. On rich soils the stems often grow too fast, becoming lax with the plant opening out in the middle. You can cut back the stems by up to half in late May to reduce this, which is known as the 'Chelsea Chop', but it's better to play to the plant's strengths by using it in those difficult drier borders.

PROPAGATION

Lift and divide clumps in spring or take cuttings in early summer. Hunt around at the base of a plant in spring and you will often find rooted pieces that are easy to snip and pot up.

WILDLIFE VALUE

These plants are magnets for autumnal hoverflies, bees and butterflies, often with several species congregating on each flower head. The flower heads last well into winter and provide shelter for insects such as ladybirds.

FASCINATING FACTS

Hylotelephium are often able to survive drought conditions due to CAM, or crassulacean acid metabolism, which simply means that the plant closes its stomata during the heat of the day to reduce water loss.

Cyclamen

Pretty, dainty and surprisingly robust

Latin name: *Cyclamen* species and varieties

Plant type: Tuberous perennial

Flower colour: Shades of pink and white

Flowering time: September to May, depending on species

Easy to grow: Yes

Height: 7–15cm (2¾–6in)

Hardy: in USDA zones 4 to 8

Planting possibilities: Beds and borders, woodland border

Growing conditions: Shade, well-drained soil, shelter from cold winds

Wildlife value: 3

GARDEN USE

There are few plants as dainty and yet as eye-catching as a cyclamen in full flower. In autumn, each tuber produces clusters of glowing pink or shining white shuttlecock flowers above mounds of beautifully silvered and marked foliage. *Cyclamen hederifolium* is the autumn-flowering species, with striking ivy-shaped leaves and flowers that can appear as early as August but are often at their best in October and November. If you want to keep the show going through the depths of winter, plant *Cyclamen coum*, which will flower from December through to March. Grow them in woodland conditions – leafy, moist soil and shade are essential, which makes them invaluable for adding autumn and winter colour to the ground under deciduous trees and shrubs after leaf fall.

HOW TO GROW

These are incredibly tough plants, bulking up over the years and living for a long time when happy. Give them shelter from strong sun and cold winds, with rich, leafy soil, and they will spread happily in clumps through the understorey. A light top dressing of leaf mould after the flowers and leaves have died back is a good idea, but other than that they tend to look after themselves.

PROPAGATION

Sow seeds in summer, although they will take a while to bulk up to flowering size. The corms don't produce offsets or divisions, so seed is really the only way to propagate cyclamen.

WILDLIFE VALUE

Small mammals, birds and ants sometimes eat the seeds of cyclamen, while bees are attracted to the flowers.

FASCINATING FACTS

Ants have a particularly close relationship with cyclamen as they do a great deal to distribute and propagate the seeds. A sticky coating attracts the ants to the seed as a foodstuff; they then carry the seed away, eat the coating and leave the seed ready to germinate in a fresh spot.

Japanese anemone

Easy, elegant and long-flowering

Latin name: *Anemone* species and varieties

Plant type: Perennial

Flower colour: Shades of pink and white

Flowering time: August to October

Easy to grow: Yes

Height: 50cm–1.2m (20in–5ft)

Hardy: in USDA zones 4 to 8

Planting possibilities: Beds and borders

Growing conditions: Sun or shade, most soils

Wildlife value: 2

GARDEN USE

With their long slender stems and delicately coloured flowers in shades of pink or white, Japanese anemones are undeniably elegant when in flower. I'm especially fond of the white forms such as 'Honorine Jobert' and 'Whirlwind' as they combine beautifully with ferns and structural evergreens, lifting a shady corner of the garden. 'Elfin Swan' is a dainty, compact form with white and mauve-blue-backed flowers that is good for damper soils, while 'Prinz Heinrich' is a rich rose-pink with a better behaved, less vigorous habit that makes it perfect for the smaller garden.

HOW TO GROW

These robust plants are easy to grow and tolerant of most soils and growing conditions, except the extremes of very wet locations or hot, dry spots. Japanese anemones are low maintenance once they're established, although they can become somewhat spreading and a touch invasive, so choose your variety and planting location carefully, and don't be afraid to keep them in check by restricting them to one area.

PROPAGATION

Divide clumps in autumn, potting them up until established, or sow the seeds as soon as they're ripe.

WILDLIFE VALUE

Bees and butterflies are attracted to the lovely golden stamens in plain view, while deer and rabbits are fortunately not interested.

FASCINATING FACTS

Despite the name, Japanese anemones are native to China but were first discovered growing in Japan by European plant hunters, hence the name.

What to do in the garden during autumn

The garden always seems to get a sudden flush of growth in early autumn, as the days begin to shorten and the weather becomes cooler and fresher. Early autumn is all about keeping the show going, and deadheading becomes my daily routine, especially for repeat flowerers such as dahlias and cosmos that are often just reaching their peak. This is one of those jobs that is such a pleasure to do, and it's also hugely rewarding as it will ensure the flowers keep on coming until the frosts stop them abruptly in their tracks.

As autumn progresses, my jobs become more attuned to preparing for the spring to come. The key task in terms of effort is undoubtedly planting bulbs of all descriptions. These range from the tiny corms of *Anemone coronaria* – a must-have for cutting – to the globes of hyacinths and alliums. I love planting bulbs in pots – miniature daffodils in old terracotta pots earlier in autumn, followed later by a rainbow of tulips in troughs and pastel-coloured glazed pots. This will be a feast for the eyes next season, and one that is wonderfully moveable, too, allowing me to create arrangements with other spring-flowering plants. Naturalizing bulbs such as crocus and narcissi into grass or using them to underplant shrubs and trees is just as rewarding, and the effort is repaid in swathes of colour come the spring.

Shorter autumnal days trigger many plants to turn to seed, which are great fun to collect for sowing the following year.

My favourite seeds to save include calendula and nigella, which are both easy to grow and will provide lots of vibrant colour next summer. Simply snip the seed heads off and dry them in paper bags, storing them in a cool, dry place ready for sowing next spring.

Collect fallen leaves and compost them separately, if you have space. The leaf mould does take a while to create as leaves rot down slowly, but it makes a wonderful soil conditioner and is an attractive mulch for borders.

Plant trees, shrubs and perennials early in autumn while the soil is still warm as they will settle in nicely before winter. You can also divide herbaceous perennials now, while the dormant period after leaf fall is the perfect time to move shrubs and trees that are in the wrong place.

Protect tender plants like *Pelargonium* and *Osteospermum* by moving them into a frost-free place if possible, or take cuttings and root them on a windowsill. Larger plants in the ground, such as *Agapanthus*, can be mulched with dry leaves or straw to protect the crown.

Planting bulbs such as daffodils is easy as they're tolerant of soil and situation and can be planted densely in pots to give a good show. Tulips are more demanding and need to be planted in the colder weather of late autumn, or they start to grow before they should. If you're planting in pots, make sure the bulbs don't touch each other as this can cause disease.

Give shrub roses a light prune in October, cutting them back to a framework. The blustery winds of autumn can play havoc with these, causing them to rock and move in the ground, making their roots vulnerable to frost damage in winter.

Winter

Gardening in the depths of winter is a challenge. It's always tempting to focus my energy on more rewarding times of the year like spring and summer, but the dreary months of deepest winter can play host to some magical flowers, lovely plant combinations and truly unforgettable scents.

Many of these winter plants are incredibly robust, despite their delicate appearance. The airy winter cherry blossom and the fragile wisps of witch hazel seem far too frail for this harsh season, yet they'll cope with the worst of the weather. As for little bulbs like snowdrops, crocuses and violas, they will often keep flowering through frost and winter storms.

Winter is a good time to have pots of dainties to hand so you can savour them from your kitchen window. I have a collection of dwarf iris, saxifrage and cyclamen that give me an ongoing show throughout the season. This might not be as spectacular as the abundance of summer, but they are little beacons of joy in the greyness of January. Detail is often what counts in winter – the intricate colouring of a viola, the purple of a speckled hellebore, the contrast of tiny, pure snowdrops with dark, leafy mulch. Add varied elements like birch bark and a few strikingly coloured dogwood stems, and you have a garden making the most of a seemingly cheerless season.

As for scent, the most spectacular fragrances waft through the winter garden, especially on a still, sunny day. The lemon perfume of winter honeysuckle, the vanilla of Christmas box and the subtle scents from a cluster of snowdrops float in the air, attracting bumblebees and eager gardeners alike to soak up the aroma.

Snowdrop

Tough, tiny and such a welcome sight

The winter garden simply isn't complete without a carpet of snowdrops. Most people are familiar with the common *Galanthus nivalis* that has naturalized throughout the UK, much of Europe and parts of the USA. It happily spreads to form a carpet through woodlands and shady field edges in winter, but there are also several other species and numerous delicately nuanced varieties that sometimes sell for a high price.

Latin name: *Galanthus* species and varieties

Plant type: Bulb

Flower colour: White and green, occasionally with some yellow touches

Flowering time: January and February

Easy to grow: Yes

Height: 7.5–20cm (3–8in)

Planting possibilities: Beds and borders, woodland border

Growing conditions: Full sun, part shade, moist soil

Wildlife value: 3

GARDEN USE

Snowdrops are an invaluable addition to the garden and, once established, will give a reliably glorious show from one year to the next with very little effort from the gardener. The easiest varieties by far are the common *Galanthus nivalis*, which is small, dainty and flowers in late January through to early March, and the robust *Galanthus* 'Atkinsii', which is bigger, bolder and flowers a little earlier, often in the first weeks of January.

Try to mimic in your garden how snowdrops grow so contentedly in the wild; think dappled shade, moist soil that is rich in organic matter, and little disturbance. They can be tricky to get settled, but persevere, trying different spots as needed. In my experience they sometimes move themselves around until they're happy, fading and dying off if the front of a border is too sunny and dry, seeding themselves and flourishing further back where it's shadier and damper. Grow them under shrubs and trees, especially those with interesting winter bark, where the whole becomes a focal point of the winter garden.

FAVOURITE SNOWDROPS

Galanthus nivalis is always adorable with its seemingly dainty leaves and flowers that are actually vigorous, sturdy and long-lasting. It's small, only 7.5cm (3in) or so tall, but so floriferous it makes up for its tiny size. Look out for the double form 'Flore/Plena' which does occur naturally but has the advantage of densely packed petals, giving a more striking appearance and turning the flowers slightly more upward.

'Atkinsii' is the easiest snowdrop I have ever grown as it seems to cope with more sun than other species and varieties. It's a big plant with strapping blue-green leaves and tall flower stems up to 20cm (8in), with correspondingly large flowers up to 2.5cm (1in) long.

'Sam Arnott' is tall with huge nodding flowers, robust to grow and great for picking for the house. It's also late flowering – towards the end of February and start of March – which extends the snowdrop season wonderfully.

'Magnet' has striking whirling flowers where the petals are flung outwards like little parachutes. They're delicately honey-fragranced and held on tall stems so they catch the breeze and move beautifully.

PLANTING PARTNERS

Snowdrops blend superbly with trees and shrubs of all sorts and the more 'woodlandy' looking, the better. Plant them with many of the shrubs in this book, such as witch hazel and winter-flowering cherry, as well as coloured-stem dogwoods, *Cornus* species and white-barked birches such as *Betula pendula* and *Betula utilis*. The sturdy *Galanthus* 'Atkinsii' makes a feature of an otherwise dull herbaceous border as long as it has room to flower freely and die back before the other plants begin to compete with it.

HOW TO GROW

Grow snowdrops under any deciduous shrubs and trees, provided the soil is rich, dense, damp and somewhat shaded. They love a rich, moisture-retentive soil in dappled sun or partial shade. Those parts of the garden that stay moist throughout spring are ideal, especially where other plants are slow to get going and won't compete with them while they're actively growing.

PROPAGATION

Snowdrops are best planted 'in the green', that is just after they have flowered, as the success rate is far higher than any other method. This means buying them from a garden centre or online, sourcing some from a friend or moving your own clusters to fit around the garden. Planting after flowering is the best way to bulk up snowdrops. It's very easy to lift and divide clumps of bulbs, replanting at once at the same level. Alternatively, sow the seeds as soon as they're ripe in spring, although the plants will take a couple of years to reach flowering size.

WILDLIFE VALUE

Snowdrops provide an early-season source of food for bees, flies and beetles. Their seeds are coated in a protein-rich compound that is attractive to ants, which carry them into their nests to feed their larvae, propagating the snowdrop at the same time.

FASCINATING FACTS

The most expensive snowdrop ever was sold in February 2022 when a single bulb of *Galanthus plicatus* 'Golden Tears' sold on eBay for £1,850 (around $2,300) plus postage.

Winter aconite

Small but bright and sunny

Latin name: *Eranthis hyemalis*

Plant type: Bulb

Flower colour: Yellow

Flowering time: February

Easy to grow: Yes

Height: 10cm (4in)

Planting possibilities: Beds and borders, woodland border

Growing conditions: Full sun, moist soil

Wildlife value: 3

GARDEN USE

This dainty little bulb is a true hero of winter, flowering its sunny little socks off right through February, just when the garden needs a lift. Happy in most soils and situations, the clear yellow flowers, backed by a 'lion's ruff' of soft green leaves, look great shining out from under the bare stems of deciduous trees and shrubs or colonizing a patch of lawn. If it's happy, it will seed and spread charmingly. In its native woodlands of France, Italy and the Balkans it makes the most of flowering when the maximum sunshine reaches the forest floor before the leaves appear on the trees, and these are the conditions it prefers in gardens. *Eranthis* look great lining the edge of a woodland path, a shrub border or dotted in a shady corner.

HOW TO GROW

Eranthis love rich, moisture-retentive soil in dappled sun or partial shade. Those parts of the garden that stay moist throughout spring are ideal.

PROPAGATION

After flowering is easiest, when it's very straightforward to lift and divide clumps of tubers, replanting at once at the same level. Alternatively, sow seed as soon as it's ripe in spring, although the plants will take a couple of years or so to reach flowering size.

WILDLIFE VALUE

Winter aconites are an important nectar source for early-flying bumblebees and other foraging insects.

FASCINATING FACTS

Wear gloves when handling winter aconites as all parts of the plant are poisonous if ingested, although it would take a large amount to cause any serious issues. However, this does mean that deer and other animals tend to leave them alone.

Christmas *or* sweet box

Unbeatable for its rich vanilla scent

Latin name: *Sarcococca*

Plant type: Evergreen shrub

Flower colour: Creamy white

Flowering time: January and February

Easy to grow: Yes

Height: 1–1.2m (3–4ft)

Planting possibilities: Beds and borders, woodland border, pots and containers

Growing conditions: Full shade, part sun, moist soil, shelter from cold winds

Wildlife value: 3

GARDEN USE

These forgiving evergreen shrubs spend most of the year looking shiny, green and rather unassuming, but once their tiny flowers start to appear in the depths of winter, the powerful vanilla scent simply stops people in their tracks. There are several species, but to my mind the prettiest is *Sarcococca confusa* with its bushy habit and black berries that follow the flowers. Plant it near a front or back door, path or gate where the scent will be unmissable. They do well in shady spots where the soil doesn't dry out, and their shiny leaves add interest. You can even clip them into box-like globes, although they're not as biddable as the hedging box and clipping does reduce the all-important flowering a little.

HOW TO GROW

Plant in autumn or spring and choose a shady, sheltered spot with moist soil. Young plants will grow well in pots for several years and can form part of an attractive winter container.

PROPAGATION

Easy to grow from stem cuttings in late summer. Make each cutting 7.5–10cm (3–4in) long and root in pots in a cold frame, potting the rooted cuttings the following spring.

WILDLIFE VALUE

The fragrant flowers provide an important nectar source for early-flying bees, while birds enjoy the berries and the shelter these dense shrubs provide.

FASCINATING FACTS

In its native China, some species of *Sarcococca* are used in traditional medicines for treating diverse conditions such as rheumatism, sore throats and traumatic injuries.

Christmas rose

Bright flowers on the darkest winter days

Latin name: *Helleborus niger*

Plant type: Perennial

Flower colour: White

Flowering time: December to March

Easy to grow: Not so easy

Height: 30–45cm (12–17¾in)

Planting possibilities: Beds and borders, woodland border, pots and containers

Growing conditions: Full shade, part sun, moist soil, shelter from cold winds

Wildlife value: 3

GARDEN USE

Among all the hellebores, the Christmas rose is the earliest to flower, by far the daintiest and definitely the most demanding species to grow. It needs a sheltered spot, soil that is neutral to alkaline, rich in lovely organic matter, and the super-early flowers often need protection with a cloche through the coldest nights. Having said all that, the flowers are charmingly more upward facing than the usual nodding flowers of most hellebore species, which makes it a great addition to winter pots and containers, especially close to the house where its dainty beauty can be best appreciated on a regular basis.

HOW TO GROW

Plant in autumn and choose a lightly shaded, sheltered spot with deep, rich, moist soil. Once planted hellebores don't like to be disturbed and the Christmas rose is more sensitive than most, so pick your spot carefully.

PROPAGATION

Sow seeds once they are ripe, usually around June, in trays or pots of sandy soil.

WILDLIFE VALUE

The flowers provide an important nectar source for early-flying bees.

FASCINATING FACTS

In the Middle Ages the Christmas rose was considered to be an elixir for eternal youth, and perhaps there is some truth in the old folklore, as nowadays it's used to treat cardiovascular problems.

Crocus

Splashes of colour take winter into spring

There is nothing that can fill a winter garden with more colour than several swathes of crocuses dotted through a lawn, under trees and anywhere they can catch your eye. The rich purples, sky blues and golden yellows stud the garden like tiny jewels, while their hardy nature makes for a good show and a long season of interest.

Latin name: *Crocus* species and varieties

Plant type: Corm

Flower colour: White, cream, yellow, blue and purple

Flowering time: February to April, although some are autumn flowering

Easy to grow: Easy

Height: 5–15cm (2–6in)

Planting possibilities: Beds and borders, woodland border, naturalized in grass, rock or gravel garden, pots and containers

Growing conditions: Full sun, part shade, moist soil

Wildlife value: 3

GARDEN USE

There are so many different ways you can use crocus species and varieties in the garden. Not only do they look great planted in window boxes, pots and containers, where their delicate colouring can be appreciated up close, but a swathe of tiny *Crocus* 'Golden Bunch' dotted across a sunny bank is a burst of winter sunshine in its own right. The three ways I tend to use crocuses are in containers for that early-season splash of rich colour, naturalized in short lawns and in rock or gravel gardens where the stone sets off the flowers beautifully.

FAVOURITE CROCUSES

***Crocus ancyrensis* or 'Golden Bunch'** is always adorable with its tiny, sunshiny yellow flowers appearing in February. Each corm produces as many as 20 flowers each, which makes for a good show.

Crocus tommasinianus is early flowering, appearing in February, and it will grow in dappled shade, seeding itself around if it's happy, which makes it a good choice for naturalizing. The species is a delicate pale mauve, but 'Whitewell Purple' and 'Ruby Giant' have a deeper, more vivid colouring.

Crocus chrysanthus types flower a little later, but the choice of colours and cultivars is wonderful. Look out for 'Cream Beauty' with brilliant orange stigmas set off against the rich cream flowers, the delicate paleness of 'Blue Pearl' and the striking striped petals of 'Gypsy Girl'. There are so many varieties to choose from that it's fun to add a couple of pots full of new ones each year.

Crocus sieberi flowers appear in February and March and there are some super varieties, including 'Violet Queen' with richly coloured flowers, and 'Tricolour' with three-toned petals of yellow, white and pale mauve.

PLANTING PARTNERS

Much like snowdrops, crocuses provide a lovely carpet of colour beneath trees and shrubs of all sorts, but unlike snowdrops, crocuses prefer well-drained soil and a sunnier spot, which makes them ideal for dotting under trees, on a sunny lawn, or in a south-facing border. Good species for lawns include *Crocus vernus* varieties and *Crocus chrysanthus* types, which are especially strong and vigorous. Avoid white forms, though, as they tend to look as if there's been an accident with a box of tissues!

Tolerating more shade, *Crocus tommasinianus* looks good combined with snowdrops and coloured-stem dogwoods, while for a dappled shade spot I love the pale mauve flowers of *Crocus sieberi*, which look great with hellebores. In borders, crocuses look wonderful dotted among smaller ornamental grasses such as *Stipa tenuissima* and *Festuca glauca*, and many of the more colourful varieties grow beautifully in rock and gravel gardens.

HOW TO GROW

Grow in full sun, unless specified, as the flowers won't open properly otherwise. However, crocuses can be naturalized in short lawns, including those with some dappled shade, as long as the lawn isn't mown until after the crocus leaves have died off later in the spring.

PROPAGATION

Grow from seed collected when the capsules ripen in July, although they will take three or four years to reach flowering size. Alternatively, lift the plants after flowering, separating off the tiny cormlets that many species produce, then grow these on until they achieve flowering size.

WILDLIFE VALUE

Crocuses are a good food source for early-flying pollinators. Unfortunately, they're also a great food source for mice, squirrels, voles and chipmunks, and it sometimes seems as if there will be no bulbs left to flower. Even so, they usually miss enough to give a good show in the garden.

FASCINATING FACTS

The spice saffron is actually the dried stigmas of the *Crocus sativus* flower, which blooms in autumn and has been cultivated for centuries. Each flower produces only three stigmas, which makes it one of the most expensive spices in the world.

Winter honeysuckle

Lemon scent stops you in your tracks

Latin name: *Lonicera fragrantissima*

Plant type: Deciduous or semi-evergreen shrub

Flower colour: White

Flowering time: December to March

Easy to grow: Easy

Height: 2m (6½ft)

Planting possibilities: Beds and borders, woodland border

Growing conditions: Full sun, part shade, any soil

Wildlife value: 4

GARDEN USE

It's easy to dismiss this somewhat ungainly shrubby honeysuckle in summer, with its fast-growing stems of rather dull green leaves. In fact, it's best treated as a backdrop shrub to other more exciting summer-flowering perennials and shrubs. But what it lacks in summer is more than made up for in winter, when those ungainly stems are studded with highly perfumed, lemon-scented, creamy white flowers in little clusters that pull in every bumblebee for miles around.

HOW TO GROW

Plant in autumn and give it room; it's a big-growing plant, although more restrained than the more easily found hybrid *Lonicera x purpusii*. These shrubs are tough and incredibly forgiving of soil and site, although they won't enjoy too shady a spot. Prune back annually in spring after flowering – you will lose some flowers the following year, but it will keep the plant within bounds.

PROPAGATION

The easiest way to propagate is by layering branches over the late summer and through the winter, weighing them down with a stone so they root into the ground over the course of a year. A quicker, though less reliable, method is by taking 10cm (4in) cuttings in July.

WILDLIFE VALUE

The highly scented flowers provide an important nectar source for early-flying bees, while birds and small mammals appreciate the shelter these dense shrubs provide.

FASCINATING FACTS

The great plant hunter Robert Fortune first introduced *Lonicera fragrantissima* to the UK from China in 1845, having discovered it on one of his expeditions for the Royal Horticultural Society. It proved so popular that only a few years later the editor of the American gardening magazine *The Horticulturist* was writing about a specimen he had been sent from the UK, and it's now a common sight throughout eastern America.

Pansy & viola

Colourful, long-flowering and cheerful

These charming little 'faces' brighten up pots and containers like nothing else. Not only are violas and pansies affordable and easy to grow, but they are also available in so many colour permutations and combinations that there should be something to please everyone.

Latin name: *Viola* species and hybrids

Plant type: Annual or herbaceous perennial

Flower colour: White, cream, yellow, orange, pink, blue and purple and variations

Flowering time: October to April, although some summer-flowering varieties

Easy to grow: Easy

Height: 5–15cm (2–6in)

Planting possibilities: Beds and borders, pots and containers, kitchen garden

Growing conditions: Full sun, part shade, any soil

Wildlife value: 2

GARDEN USE

If you're only going to buy one winter plant from this book, make it a handful of violas and you won't be sorry. There is simply no plant that flowers for longer, albeit somewhat intermittently, from autumn all the way through to the following spring and sometimes beyond. Use dainty little violas in all sorts of pots and containers, on their own or, even better, with other winter plants such as hellebores and with spring-flowering bulbs like dwarf daffodils. Plant the larger flowering pansies dotted in borders, bigger planters or in a swathe to brighten up a dull path. Whatever you use them for, they'll look super sweet and will enhance your winter garden no end.

FAVOURITE VIOLAS AND PANSIES

Viola 'Antique Shades' has dainty flowers in a delicate mix of copper and smoky pink-purple that have the ability to blend with almost any other colours.

Viola 'Sorbet' series is so reliable and encompasses a range of brilliant colours from pure white to deepest black, including the rather marvellous 'Phantom' with rich, velvet-purple flowers. 'Yesterday, Today and Tomorrow' is a mix of white, ice-blue and pale blue flowers carefully selected to blend beautifully together.

Viola 'Honeybee' has warm golden-yellow flowers tinged with copper and brown.

Pansy 'Panola' series has smaller flowers than many other pansy varieties but produces a good number through the winter months that stand up to the weather well. Look for 'Beaconsfield' with deep purple lower petals and lavender upper petals, or 'Fire' with velvet orange-red flowers.

Pansy 'Cool Wave' series has a trailing habit that is bred especially for hanging baskets and planters. 'Blueberry Swirl' has soft blue and creamy yellow two-tone flowers, while 'Frost' has delicate white and ice-blue flowers centred with a golden yellow eye.

PLANTING PARTNERS

Pansies and violas go well with almost anything. Plant them with bulbs and other winter flowers in the border, using them to add interest and provide ground cover under trees and shrubs. Dot a few plants into a rock garden or a planting of grasses to add a splash of colour. Violas and trailing pansies are especially good in window boxes and hanging baskets, and you'll often get the best show from planting them in pots and containers where the flowers can be appreciated at eye level.

HOW TO GROW

Pansies and violas are easy to grow provided the soil doesn't get too waterlogged, so make sure any pots and boxes have suitable drainage. They like a partially shaded site but will be happy in full sun as long as they don't get too hot. The crucial thing is to keep deadheading regularly as this will ensure the plants keep on flowering.

PROPAGATION

Sow seeds in summer or take 3–5cm (1¼–2in) cuttings of non-flowering shoots in July.

WILDLIFE VALUE

Hybrid varieties of pansy and viola are of little benefit to wildlife as they have been bred for long flowering and have little nectar or pollen.

FASCINATING FACTS

The wild form of viola, *Viola tricolor*, is surrounded by herbal folklore. Its common name of heartsease stems from the belief that it could ease a broken heart, while myth has it that all violas were originally white until they were pierced by Cupid's arrow, giving them their colours and the magic to create love potions.

LIMITED

Witch hazel

Small flowers that pack a colourful punch

Latin name: *Hamamelis*

Plant type: Deciduous shrub or small tree

Flower colour: Yellow, orange or red

Flowering time: January to March

Easy to grow: Requires a good site and soil

Height: 2–3m (6½–10ft)

Planting possibilities: Beds and borders, woodland border

Growing conditions: Part sun, moist soil, shelter from cold winds

Wildlife value: 2

GARDEN USE

There is something ethereal about the spidery, often scented flowers of witch hazel. Looking far too dainty and delicate to withstand the weather of January, February and March, these shrubs are actually incredibly hardy and will even cope with more air pollution than many plants. Treat them as a true specimen plant, giving it pride of place in a woodland planting, shrub border or as a stand-alone single small tree. Not only do the winter flowers stand out surprisingly brightly given their small size, but the autumn foliage colours are outstanding, too.

HOW TO GROW

Plant in autumn in neutral to acidic soil in a dappled, shaded spot that is sheltered from cold winds.

PROPAGATION

This is not the easiest of plants to propagate but you can achieve success, albeit slowly, by layering branches over the late summer and through the winter, although this can take a couple of years or more. Alternatively, take heel cuttings in late summer, although this method is very hit and miss. It's far easier to buy a grown plant, recognizing that its expense is down to the difficulty of propagation.

WILDLIFE VALUE

Birds and small mammals eat the fruit capsules and seeds.

FASCINATING FACTS

The common name witch hazel derives from the practice of using the forked twigs to find water by dowsing or 'water witching'.

Winter cherry

A dainty tree with flowers in the depths of winter

Latin name: *Prunus subhirtella* 'Autumnalis' or 'Autumnalis Rosea'

Plant type: Deciduous small tree

Flower colour: White or soft pink

Flowering time: November to March

Easy to grow: Yes, in good conditions

Height: 6–9m (20–29½ft)

Planting possibilities: Beds and borders, woodland border

Growing conditions: Full sun, well-drained soil, shelter from cold winds

Wildlife value: 2

GARDEN USE

The winter cherry tree is a true star of the winter, flowering intermittently but persistently throughout. The flowers are pure white or a delicate pink, depending on the variety, semi-double and around 2cm (¾in) wide, standing out against the dark, bare branches strikingly. It makes a great tree for smaller gardens with its elegant habit, and the flowers stud the bare stems, brightening up the garden in the depths of winter. As with all cherries, the leaves turn attractive autumnal shades of red, yellow and orange. These combined attributes make it an ideal stand-alone tree for a special spot – just make sure you can appreciate it in all its glory throughout the winter.

HOW TO GROW

Like all cherries, the winter cherry prefers well-drained, but not dry, soil, so avoid heavy clay or any waterlogged spots. Also make sure it's sheltered from wind to protect the flowers.

PROPAGATION

It's best to buy a ready-grown tree, as cultivated named varieties like these can only be grown from cuttings of a parent plant, which are then frequently grafted onto a rootstock.

WILDLIFE VALUE

The winter flowers provide a vital source of nectar and pollen for insects, while the twiggy foliage makes a great habitat for birds in summer.

FASCINATING FACTS

In Japanese culture, the winter cherry is associated with the concept of *mono no aware*, which is translated as 'the beauty of transience'. The fleeting blossom in the bleak winter months embodies an appreciation for brief moments of beauty.

Lenten rose

Charmingly speckled cream, pink or purple flowers

Latin name: *Helleborus orientalis*

Plant type: Herbaceous perennial

Flower colour: White, cream, pink or purple

Flowering time: February to April

Easy to grow: Yes

Height: 45–55cm (17¾–21½in)

Planting possibilities: Beds and borders, woodland border

Growing conditions: Full sun, full and part shade, moist soil

Wildlife value: 3

GARDEN USE

Despite its name this charming little plant is not a rose, but don't be fooled by its diminutive size because it's one of the toughest, hardiest plants you can grow in your garden. Flowering in the worst of the winter months, the flower stems are often frozen by frost, splaying them down to the ground in an alarming fashion. But, given some warmth and sunshine, they soon defrost, becoming upright again as the day progresses, as if nothing had ever happened to them. This plant is highly variable and that is a key part of its charm. The colours vary from pure white through buttermilk to rich, dark burgundy-purples, often with random speckling on the petals but sometimes with none whatsoever. All are lovely forms and seedlings can be any variation. There are some named selections and hybrids, which are often very expensive to buy, but I think the 'lucky dip' nature of the species is far more fun and interesting in the garden. Use them en masse as ground cover under trees or dot plants into borders to add interest during the winter months.

HOW TO GROW

These are the most forgiving hellebores to grow, thriving in shade, dappled sun or even full sun as long as the soil is deep, moist and rich in organic matter. De-leaf in December to allow the flowers to shine but also to reduce the chance of a disfiguring leaf spot, which often affects hellebores.

PROPAGATION

Lenten rose is so easy to grow from seed sown as soon as they ripen in June. In fact, if you have plants near a gravel path, you'll find the path acts as a perfect seedbed, where you can simply lift and pot up plantlets later in the summer. These will flower when they're two or three years old.

WILDLIFE VALUE

The abundant flowers are good for bees and other pollinators, while happily they are also unattractive to deer and rabbits.

FASCINATING FACTS

Lenten rose flowers are exceptionally long-lasting, even when cut for the house. In the garden they can last for up to three months because the petals are actually sepals and are much tougher than delicate petals. As the season wears on these darken, becoming tougher and coarser as the seeds develop.

What to do in the garden during winter

My favourite job in December is to make a wreath for the front door. This is such a fun and creative thing to do, and easier than you might think. The winter garden is full of so many great things that will make it unique: fruits, foliage and flower heads of all kinds.

Early winter is all about tidying up: cutting back and mulching dahlias if you leave them in the ground, or lifting and storing them if you don't; potting and planting the last of the bulbs that are still hanging about in their packets; and putting the garden to bed for the winter.

After the holidays there's all the pruning and tying in to be done. Wisteria, trained roses, vines, and apple and pear espaliers can all be pruned into their place during these darker days. Milder days are perfect for moving shrubs and larger plants around the garden or planting new ones. Larger plants prefer the chance to settle in over the winter, getting their roots down with the soil nicely bedded in around them before the growing kicks off in the spring.

On those absolutely freezing days when there really is nothing to be done outside, spend some time planning. Get your seed order together, plan that cut flower border you want to plant in spring and browse through your books, magazines and catalogues, giving your imagination free rein.

By now your dahlias will have gone over and will need cutting back to 10cm (4in) or so. If you're in a milder area, you may be able to leave your dahlias in the ground, top dressing with a good mulch of garden compost, but I've always found they're irresistible to slugs as they start to grow in the spring. In my experience it's best to lift them, dry them off for a week or two and then pot them up into dry compost to store for the winter, planting them out again in late spring once they're actively growing, larger plants.

Finish off planting any bulbs you have left on those milder days of December and early January. This is an easy job if you're planting in pots, but if you're planting into the ground it needs to be unfrozen and not too sodden.

Check your pots and containers to make sure they're moist every now and then. Containerized plants can dry out in winter, especially after a spell of freezing weather. Make sure to lift them onto pot feet, bricks or lathes of wood so they can drain properly in the wet weather too.

Prune climbing roses, wisteria and vines by cutting away any dead, diseased or damaged wood, shaping the plant to a framework as you cut. Vines and wisteria grow a lot in one season, so don't be afraid to keep them in check.

Protect the crowns of potentially vulnerable plants such as *Agapanthus, Hedychium* and *Melianthus* with a top dressing of bark chips. Alternatively, use leaves or bracken netted down with fleece or chicken wire to keep them in place, which also works well for tender plants in pots.

Don't forget to feed the birds during this bleak winter period, cleaning your feeders regularly to reduce the chance of disease.

Index of common names

Index of Latin names

Index of flower colours

White

Pink

Blue

Purple

Yellow

Red

Orange

Index of plant types

Bulbs, corms and tubers

Annuals and biennials

Herbaceous perennials

Acknowledgements

My name might be on the cover, but a book is a hugely collaborative endeavour with many people involved in getting the final copy onto a bookshelf. Many thanks to James whose wonderful illustrations bring my words to life so beautifully and evocatively. A huge thanks to Maeve for designing this lovely book. I'm so lucky to have worked with these two on many collaborations and I can't thank you both enough for your skills and artistry.

I'm so grateful to Harriet and the Quadrille team for being such a joy to work with, as always. This is the sixth book we've worked on together and hopefully there will be many more. Likewise, I can't thank Jane and Amy at Graham Maw Christie enough for all they do and for taking me on in the first place.

My mum's support was invaluable in whittling down the list to just 52 flowers, phoning me to suggest new ones and insisting that I keep forsythia because so many people love it. Finally, thanks must go to Paul, my rock of patience, for checking my copy thoroughly and reading every word, including these, to make sure it all makes sense.

Quadrille, Penguin Random House UK,
One Embassy Gardens, 8 Viaduct Gardens,
London SW11 7BW

Quadrille Publishing Limited is part of the Penguin Random House group of companies whose addresses can be found at global.penguinrandomhouse.com

Published by Quadrille in 2025

www.penguin.co.uk

A CIP catalogue record for this book is available from the British Library

ISBN 978 1 83783 426 6
10 9 8 7 6 5 4 3 2 1

Managing Director Sarah Lavelle
Publishing Director Kate Pollard
Editorial Director Harriet Butt
Assistant Editor Harriet Thornley
Designer Maeve Bargman
Illustrator James Weston Lewis
Head of Production Stephen Lang
Production Controller Sumayyah Waheed

Colour reproduction by p2d

Printed in China by RR Donnelley Asia Printing Solutions Limited

The authorized representative in the EEA is Penguin Random House Ireland, Morrison Chambers, 32 Nassau Street, Dublin D02 YH68.

MIX
Paper | Supporting responsible forestry
FSC® C018179

Penguin Random House is committed to a sustainable future for our business, our readers and our planet. This book is made from Forest Stewardship Council® certified paper.